Big Book of Seasons, Holidays, and Weather

# Big Book of Seasons, Holidays, and Weather

## Rhymes, Fingerplays, and Songs for Children

Elizabeth Cothen Low

AN IMPRINT OF ABC-CLIO, LLC
Santa Barbara, California • Denver, Colorado • Oxford, England

**Library of Congress Cataloging-in-Publication Data**

Big book of seasons, holidays, and weather : rhymes, fingerplays, and songs for children / [compiled by]
    Elizabeth C. Low.
      p. cm.
    Includes bibliographical references and index.
    ISBN 978-1-59884-623-2 (pbk.) -- ISBN 978-1-59884-624-9 (ebook)
  1. Seasons--Juvenile poetry. 2. Holidays--Juvenile poetry. 3. Weather--Juvenile poetry. 4. Time--Juvenile poetry. 5. Children's poetry, English. 6. Children's poetry, American. 7. Nursery rhymes. 8. Finger play. 9. Children's songs, English. 10. Children's libraries--Activity programs. I. Low, Elizabeth Cothen, 1977-
PR1195.S42B54 2011
    577.2'3--dc23          2011028619

ISBN: 978-1-59884-623-2
EISBN: 978-1-59884-624-9

15  14  13  12  11    1  2  3  4  5

This book is also available on the World Wide Web as an eBook.
Visit www.abc-clio.com for details.

Libraries Unlimited
An Imprint of ABC-CLIO, LLC

ABC-CLIO, LLC
130 Cremona Drive, P.O. Box 1911
Santa Barbara, California 93116-1911

This book is printed on acid-free paper ∞
Manufactured in the United States of America

# Contents

## Part 2: Time

# Acknowledgments

Thank you to Barbara Ittner for giving me a chance to do this second book and for working with me on it so patiently. Thanks also to my family for their tireless support and ideas.

# Introduction

Rhymes, fingerplays, and songs have long been important tools for educating children. Throughout history, lullabies and rhymes have been used first to soothe and then to stimulate very small children. Through wordplay, children learn about vocabulary, sentence structure, and relationships between words. They come to appreciate the richness of language, the ways in which words can be combined to create meaning. As they develop, rhymes and poems help children acquire a sense of history and place. Fingerplays and action rhymes (rhymes with accompanying finger and hand movements) also build physical coordination, as well as provide mental stimulation. Nursery songs introduce basic melodies and provide a basis for later music appreciation. But most important, rhymes and songs encourage a love of language and foster imaginative thinking.

With this in mind, two years ago I published a volume called *Big Book of Animal Rhymes, Fingerplays, and Songs*, a comprehensive compilation of rhymes, fingerplays, songs, and poems intended for librarians and educators to use with children from infancy through middle school. This volume is a follow-up to that one, but instead of focusing on animals as a subject, it deals with the seasons, weather, and time. This book is intended to help anyone who works with children find interesting and age-appropriate material to enrich programming or curriculum. Included are a total of 294 entries. The text also features musical notations for 32 songs and instructions for performing 44 action rhymes and fingerplays. It is my hope that this collection will be useful for children's librarians, teachers, and childcare providers interested in thematic programming, as well as a reference tool for librarians and patrons seeking fingerplays, action rhymes, nursery rhymes, songs, and poems about the seasons.

## Organization

This book is divided into two parts: "The Four Seasons" and "Time." Within part 1 is a chapter about the four seasons and weather in general, followed by separate chapters about spring, summer, autumn, and winter. These chapters are further divided into sections, such as "Spring Weather: Rain" or "Autumn Holidays: Thanksgiving." To assist educators, I have also noted the type and age range for each entry. Definitions for the more archaic terms used are listed after the relevant entries. Part 2 includes chapters on time other than seasons and months.

## Types of Entries

Here are the types of entries included in this book:

- **Action rhyme:** A rhyme that has accompanying hand and body motions.

- **Fingerplay:** A rhyme that has accompanying hand motions.

- **Nursery rhyme:** For the purposes of this book, an anonymous rhyme that is intended for young children.

- **Poem:** For the purposes of this book, an authored rhyme or a longer anonymous rhyme.

- **Riddle:** A puzzling question with an answer.

- **Saying:** A short rhyme based on superstitious beliefs.

- **Song:** A rhyme that has accompanying music.

## Age Ranges

Older infants and toddlers love bouncing rhymes and toe-counting rhymes. Preschoolers enjoy learning fingerplays and acting out simple rhymes, as well as singing funny songs. Grade schoolers are ready for more complex rhymes, such as tongue-twisters, and teens can appreciate rhymes and poems with more sophisticated content, such as satire, and vocabulary. I have included the following age guidelines:

B/T     Babies/Toddlers

PreS    Preschool

K–5     Kindergarten–5th grade

6+      6th grade and above

# Methodology and Copyright Issues

I used a wide variety of print and electronic sources for this project, including books, databases, indexes, and Web sites. In some cases, I found numerous versions of the same rhyme. I tried to use the most common version (or the most appropriate for children.) If I could not find a prevalent version, I merged together several variations. All of the entries in this book are thoroughly cross-referenced, so that, for example, all entries that mention snow are referenced in the "Winter Weather: Snow" section. I have also been extremely careful to only include works that are not currently under copyright. I was able to use a number of pre-1922 sources, which are in the public domain in the United States, for most of the nursery rhymes, songs, and poems. Fingerplays and action rhymes are trickier, because many have been passed around for decades in the oral tradition, without any clue to authorship. Regardless, I did not include anything in this collection that I did not find published at least three times without any information about authorship (unless the source itself was known to be in the public domain). I also did not include musical notation unless I had access to several scores with similar melodies or was able to piece out the melody myself. Any inclusion of copyrighted material is completely unintentional and will be corrected in future editions. All instructions for fingerplays and action rhymes have been written or adapted by me.

# Part 1

---

## The Four Seasons

The entries in the first chapter in this section relate to two or more seasons. They also include different types of weather patterns. The other four chapters each cover one season: spring, summer, autumn, and winter.

# The Four Seasons

## Cuckoo, Cuckoo (Traditional, Nursery Rhyme, PreS/K–5)

Cuckoo, cuckoo,
What do you do?
In April,
I open my bill;
In May,
I sing night and day;
In June,
I change my tune;
In July,
Away I fly;
In August,
Away I must.

## The Cuckoo Comes in April (Traditional, Nursery Rhyme, PreS/K–5)

The cuckoo comes in April,
Stops all the month of May,
Sings a song at Midsummer,
And then he goes away.

From *Big Book of Seasons, Holidays, and Weather: Rhymes, Fingerplays, and Songs for Children* by Elizabeth Cothen Low. Santa Barbara, CA: Libraries Unlimited. Copyright © 2011.

## The Fairybook (Norman Gale, Poem, K–5/6+)

In summer, when the grass is thick, if mother has the time,
She shows me with her pencil how a poet makes a rhyme,
And often she is sweet enough to choose a leafy nook,
Where I cuddle up so closely when she reads the Fairybook.

In winter, when the corn's asleep, and birds are not in song,
And crocuses and violets have been away too long,
Dear mother puts her thimble by in answer to my look,
And I cuddle up so closely when she reads the Fairybook.

And mother tells the servants that of course they must contrive
To manage all the household things from four till half-past five,
For we really cannot suffer interruption from the cook,
When we cuddle close together with the happy Fairybook.

## The Garden Year (Sara Coleridge, Poem, K–5/6+)

January brings the snow,
Makes our feet and fingers glow.

February brings the rain,
Thaws the frozen lake again.

March brings breezes, loud and shrill,
To stir the dancing daffodil.

April brings the primrose sweet,
Scatters daisies at our feet.

May brings flocks of pretty lambs
Skipping by their fleecy dams.

June brings tulips, lilies, roses,
Fills the children's hands with posies.

Hot July brings cooling showers,
Apricots, and gillyflowers.

August brings the sheaves of corn,
Then the harvest home is borne.

Warm September brings the fruit;
Sportsmen then begin to shoot.

Fresh October brings the pheasant;
Then to gather nuts is pleasant.

Dull November brings the blast;
Then the leaves are whirling fast.

Chill December brings the sleet,
Blazing fire, and Christmas treat.

## The Human Seasons (John Keats, Poem, 6+)

Four Seasons fill the measure of the year;
There are four seasons in the mind of man:
He has his lusty Spring, when fancy clear
Takes in all beauty with an easy span:

He has his Summer, when luxuriously
Spring's honeyed cud of youthful thought he loves
To ruminate, and by such dreaming high
Is nearest unto Heaven: quiet coves

His soul has in its Autumn, when his wings
He furleth close; contented so to look
On mists in idleness—to let fair things
Pass by unheeded as a threshold brook:—

He has his Winter too of pale misfeature,
Or else he would forego his mortal nature.

## January Cold Desolate (Christina Rossetti, Poem, K–5/6+)

January cold desolate;
February all dripping wet;
March wind ranges;
April changes;
Birds sing in tune
To flowers of May,
And sunny June
Brings longest day;

In scorched July
The storm-clouds fly
Lightning-torn;
August bears corn,
September fruit;
In rough October
Earth must disrobe her;
Stars fall and shoot
In keen November;
And night is long
And cold is strong
In bleak December.

## Lazy Lawrence (Traditional, Nursery Rhyme, PreS/K–5)

Lazy Lawrence, let me go,
Don't hold me summer and winter too.

## On the First of March (Traditional, Nursery Rhyme, K–5/6+)

On the first of March,
The crows begin to search;
On the first of April
They are sitting still;
By the first of May
They've all flown away,
Coming greedy back again
With October's wind and rain.

## The Seasons (Traditional, Nursery Rhyme, K–5/6+)

Spring is showery, flowery, bowery;
Summer is hoppy, croppy, poppy;
Autumn is wheezy, sneezy, freezy;
Winter is slippy, drippy, nippy.

## A Swarm of Bees in May (Traditional, Nursery Rhyme, K–5/6+)

A swarm of bees in May,
Is worth a load of hay;
A swarm of bees in June,
Is worth a silver spoon;
A swarm of bees in July,
Isn't worth a fly.

## Thirty Days Hath September (Traditional, Nursery Rhyme, K–5/6+)

Thirty days hath September,
April, June, and November;
February has twenty-eight alone,
All the rest have thirty-one,
Excepting leap-year, that's the time
When February's days are twenty-nine.

## Young and Old (Charles Kingsley, Poem, 6+)

When all the world is young, lad,
And all the trees are green;
And every goose a swan, lad,
And every lass a queen;
Then hey for boot and horse, lad,
And round the world away;
Young blood must have its course, lad,
And every dog his day.

When all the world is old, lad,
And all the trees are brown;
And all the sport is stale, lad,
And all the wheels run down;
Creep home, and take your place there,
The spent and maimed among;
God grant you find one face there
You loved when all was young.

# The Four Seasons: Weather

## Children's Song (Ford Madox Ford, Poem, 6+)

Sometimes wind and sometimes rain,
Then the sun comes back again;
Sometimes rain and sometimes snow,
Goodness, how we'd like to know
Why the weather alters so.

When the weather's really good
We go nutting in the wood;
When it rains we stay at home,
And then sometimes other some
Of the neighbors' children come.

Sometimes we have jam and meat,
All the things we like to eat;
Sometimes we make do with bread
And potatoes boiled instead.
Once when we were put to bed
We had naught and mother cried,
But that was after father died.

So, sometimes wind and sometimes rain,
Then the sun comes back again;
Sometimes rain and sometimes snow,
Goodness, how we'd like to know
If things will always alter so.

## The Evening Red (Traditional, Saying, K–5/6+)

The evening red, and the morning gray,
Are the tokens of a bonny day.

## If All the Raindrops (Traditional, Song, PreS/K–5)

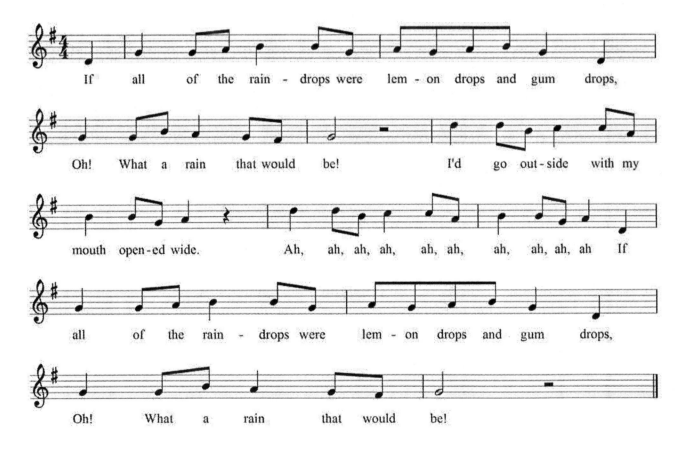

From *Big Book of Seasons, Holidays, and Weather: Rhymes, Fingerplays, and Songs for Children* by Elizabeth Cothen Low. Santa Barbara, CA: Libraries Unlimited. Copyright © 2011.

Verse 2: If all the raindrops
Were lemondrops and gumdrops,
Oh, what a rain that would be!
Standing outside, with my mouth open wide,
Ah, ah, ah, ah, ah, ah, ah, ah, ah, ah!
If all the raindrops
Were lemondrops and gumdrops,
Oh, what a rain that would be!

Verse 3: If all the snowflakes
Were candy bars and milkshakes,
Oh, what a snow that would be!
Standing outside, with my mouth open wide,
Ah, ah, ah, ah, ah, ah, ah, ah, ah, ah!
If all the snowflakes
Were candy bars and milkshakes,
Oh, what a snow that would be!

Verse 4: If all the sunbeams
Were bubblegum and ice cream,
Oh, what a sun that would be!
Standing outside, with my mouth open wide,
Ah, ah, ah, ah, ah, ah, ah, ah, ah, ah!
If all the sunbeams
Were bubblegum and ice cream,
Oh, what a sun that would be!

## A Red Sky at Night (Traditional, Saying, K–5/6+)

A red sky at night is a shepherd's delight;
A red sky in the morning is a shepherd's warning.

## Round the House (Traditional, Nursery Rhyme, PreS/K–5)

Round the house, and round the house,
And there lies a white glove* in the window.
Round the house, and round the house,
And there lies a black glove* in the window.

*"White glove" means snow; "black glove" means rain.

From *Big Book of Seasons, Holidays, and Weather: Rhymes, Fingerplays, and Songs for Children* by Elizabeth Cothen Low. Santa Barbara, CA: Libraries Unlimited. Copyright © 2011.

## Sing, Little Bird (Traditional, Nursery Rhyme, PreS/K–5)

Sing, little bird, when the skies are blue,
Sing, for the world has need of you,
Sing when the skies are overcast,
Sing when the rain is falling fast.
Sing, happy heart, when the sun is warm,
Sing in the winter's coldest storm,
Sing little songs, O heart so true,
Sing, for the world has need of you.

# Spring

## Answer to a Child's Question (Samuel Taylor Coleridge, Poem, 6+)

Do you ask what the birds say? The Sparrow, the Dove,
The Linnet and Thrush say, "I love and I love!"
In the winter they're silent—the wind is so strong;
What it says, I don't know, but it sings a loud song.
But green leaves, and blossoms, and sunny warm weather,
And singing, and loving—all come back together.
But the Lark is so brimful of gladness and love,
The green fields below him, the blue sky above,
That he sings, and he sings, and forever sings he—
"I love my Love, and my Love loves me!"

## The Bluebird (Emily Huntington Miller, Poem, K–5/6+)

I know the song that the bluebird is singing,
Up in the apple tree, where he is swinging.
Brave little fellow! the skies may be dreary,
Nothing cares he while his heart is so cheery.
 Hark! how the music leaps out from his throat!

Hark! was there ever so merry a note?
Listen awhile, and you'll hear what he's saying,
Up in the apple tree, swinging and swaying.

Dear little blossoms, down under the snow,
You must be weary of winter, I know;
Hark! while I sing you a message of cheer,
Summer is coming and springtime is here!

Little white snowdrop, I pray you arise;
Bright yellow crocus, come, open your eyes;
Sweet little violets hid from the cold,
Put on your mantles of purple and gold;
Daffodils, daffodils! say, do you hear?
Summer is coming, and springtime is here!

## Child's Song in Spring (Edith Nesbit, Poem, 6+)

The silver birch is a dainty lady,
She wears a satin gown;
The elm tree makes the old churchyard shady,
She will not live in town.

The English oak is a sturdy fellow,
He gets his green coat late;
The willow is smart in a suit of yellow,
While brown the beech trees wait.
 Such a gay green gown God gives the larches—
As green as He is good!
The hazels hold up their arms for arches
When Spring rides through the wood.
 The chestnut's proud, and the lilac's pretty,
The poplar's gentle and tall,
But the plane tree's kind to the poor dull city—
I love him best of all!

## The Coming of Spring (Traditional, Poem, K–5/6+)

The birds are coming home soon;
I look for them every day;
I listen to catch the first wild strain, For they must be singing by May.
The bluebird, he'll come first, you know,

From *Big Book of Seasons, Holidays, and Weather: Rhymes, Fingerplays, and Songs for Children*
by Elizabeth Cothen Low. Santa Barbara, CA: Libraries Unlimited. Copyright © 2011.

Like a violet that has taken wings;
And the red-breast trills while his nest he builds;
I can hum the song that he sings.

And the crocus and wind flower are coming, too;
They're already upon the way;
When the sun warms the brown earth through and through,
I shall look for them any day.
Then be patient, and wait a little, my dear;
"They're coming," the winds repeat;
"We're coming! we're coming!" I'm sure I hear,
From the grass blades that grow at my feet.

## Cuckoo! (Traditional, Song, K–5/6+)

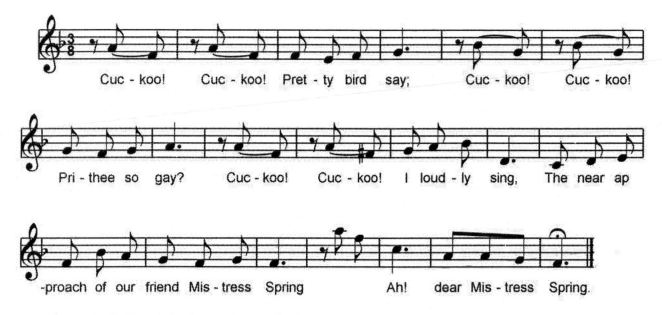

Verse 2: Cuckoo! Cuckoo! You at the best,
Cuckoo! Cuckoo! Are but a guest,
Cuckoo! Cuckoo! No sooner here
Than you are gone, till the following year.
Ah! Gone till next year.

Verse 3: Cuckoo! Cuckoo! We almost cry.
Cuckoo! Cuckoo! Saying good-bye!
Cuckoo! Cuckoo! Promise, dear, do,
Not to forget us; we shan't forget you!
Ah! Cuckoo! Adieu!

*See also* "Cuckoo, Cuckoo" (Traditional, PreS/K–5) in "The Four Seasons" chapter.
*See also* "The Cuckoo Comes in April" (Traditional, PreS/K–5) in "The Four Seasons" chapter.

## The Days Are Clear (Christina Rossetti, Poem, K–5/6+)

The days are clear,
Day after day,
When April's here,
That leads to May,
And June
Must follow soon:
Stay, June, stay!—
If only we could stop the moon
And June!

## Fairy Song (John Keats, Poem, 6+)*

Shed no tear! O, shed no tear!
The flower will bloom another year.
Weep no more! O, weep no more!
Young buds sleep in the root's white core.
Dry your eyes! O, dry your eyes!
For I was taught in Paradise
To ease my breast of melodies,—
Shed no tear.

Overhead! look overhead!
'Mong the blossoms white and red,—
Look up, look up! I flutter now
On this flush pomegranate bough.
See me! 'tis this silvery bill
Ever cures the good man's ill,—
Shed no tear! O, shed no tear!
The flower will bloom another year.
Adieu, adieu—I fly—adieu!
I vanish in the heaven's blue,—
Adieu, adieu!

*See also* "The Garden Year" (Sara Coleridge, K–5/6+) in "The Four Seasons" chapter.

## The Gladness of Nature (William Cullen Bryant, Poem, 6+)

Is this a time to be cloudy and sad,
When our mother Nature laughs around;
When even the deep blue heavens look glad,
And gladness breathes from the blossoming ground?

14

There are notes of joy from the hang-bird and wren,
And the gossip of swallows through all the sky;
The ground-squirrel gaily chirps by his den,
And the wilding bee hums merrily by.

The clouds are at play in the azure space
And their shadows at play on the bright-green vale,
And here they stretch to the frolic chase,
And there they roll on the easy gale.

There's a dance of leaves in that aspen bower,
There's a titter of winds in that beechen tree,
There's a smile on the fruit, and a smile on the flower,
And a laugh from the brook that runs to the sea.

And look at the broad-faced sun, how he smiles
On the dewy earth that smiles in his ray,
On the leaping waters and gay young isles;
Ay, look, and he'll smile thy gloom away.

See also "The Human Seasons" (John Keats, 6+) in "The Four Seasons" chapter.

## I Am a Little Toad Staying By the Road (Traditional, Action Rhyme, PreS/K–5)

I am a little toad
Staying by the road.
Just listen to my song; (Cup hand around ear.)
I sleep all winter long. (Put hands together and rest hands on head.)
When spring comes, I peek out, (Place hand above eyes and look underneath.)
And then I jump about; (Jump.)
And now I catch a fly. (Stick out tongue.)
And now I wink my eye, (Wink eye.)
And now and then I hop. (Hop.)
And now and then I stop. (Stop, return to seat.)

## In the Month of February (Traditional, Nursery Rhyme, PreS/K–5)

In the month of February,
When green leaves begin to spring,
Little lambs do skip like fairies,
Birds do couple, build, and sing.

## In March (Traditional, Nursery Rhyme, K–5/6+)

In March
The birds begin to search;
In April
The corn begins to fill;
In May
The birds begin to lay.

## Intery, Mintery, Cutery-Corn (Traditional, Counting-Out Rhyme, PreS/K–5)

Intery, mintery, cutery-corn,
Apple seed and apple thorn;
Wine, brier, limber-lock,
Five geese in a flock,
Sing and sing by a spring,
O-U-T, and in again.

*See also* "January Cold Desolate" (Christina Rossetti, K–5/6+) in "The Four Seasons" chapter.

## March Winds (Traditional, Saying, PreS/K–5)

March winds and April showers,
Bring forth May flowers.

## March Will Search (Traditional, Saying, K–5/6+)

March will search, April will try,
May will tell ye if ye'll live or die.

## Minnie and Mattie (Christina Rossetti, Poem, K–5/6+)

Minnie and Mattie
And fat little May,
Out in the country,
Spending a day.
Such a bright day,
With the sun glowing,
And the trees half in leaf,
And the grass growing.

Pinky-white pigling
Squeals through his snout,
Woolly-white lambkin
Frisks all about.
Cluck! Cluck! the nursing hen
Summons her folk,—
Ducklings all downy soft,
Yellow as yolk.
Cluck! Cluck! the mother hen
Summons her chickens
To peck the dainty bits
Found in her pickings.

Minnie and Mattie
And May carry posies,
Half of sweet violets,
Half of primroses.
Give the sun time enough,
Glowing and glowing,
He'll rouse the roses
And bring them blowing.

Don't wait for roses,
Losing to-day, O Minnie, O Mattie,
And wise little May.
Violets and primroses
Blossom to-day,
For Minnie and Mattie
And fat little May.

*See also* "On the First of March" (Traditional, K–5/6+) in "The Four Seasons" chapter.

## Sir Robin (Lucy Larcom, Poem, K–5/6+)

Rollicking Robin is here again.
What does he care for the April rain?
Care for it? Glad of it! Doesn't he know
That the April rain carries off the snow,
And coaxes out leaves to shadow his nest,
And washes his pretty red Easter vest!
And makes the juice of the cherry sweet,
For his hungry little robins to eat?
"Ha! ha! ha!" Hear the jolly bird laugh.
"That isn't the best of the story, by half."

*See also* "The Seasons" (Traditional, K–5/6+) in "The Four Seasons" chapter.
*See also* "A Swarm of Bees in May" (Traditional, K–5/6+) in "The Four Seasons" chapter.
*See also* "Thirty Days Hath September" (Traditional, K–5, 6+) in "The Four Seasons" chapter.

## The Visitor (Patrick R. Chalmers, Poem, 6+)

The white goat Amaryllis,
She wandered at her will
At time of daffodillies
Afar and up the hill:
We hunted and we holloa'd
And back she came at dawn,
But what d'you think had followed?—
A little, pagan Faun!

His face was like a berry.
His ears were high and pricked:
Tip-tap—his hoofs came merry
As up the path he clicked;
A junket for his winning
We set in dairy delf;
He eat it—peart and grinning
As Christian as yourself!

He stayed about the steading
A fortnight, say, or more;
A blanket for his bedding
We spread beside the door;
And when the cocks crowed clearly
Before the dawn was ripe,
He'd call the milkmaids cheerly
Upon a reedy pipe!

That fortnight of his staying
The work went smooth as silk:
The hens were all in laying,
The cows were all in milk;
And then—and then one morning
The maids woke up at day
Without his oaten warning,—
And found he'd gone away.

He left no trace behind him;
But still the milkmaids deem
That they, perhaps, may find him
With butter and with cream:
Beside the door they set them
In bowl and golden pat,

But no one comes to get them—
Unless, maybe, the cat.

The white goat Amaryllis,
She wanders at her will
At time of daffodillies,
Away up Woolcombe hill;
She stays until the morrow,
Then back she comes at dawn;
But never—to our sorrow—
The little, pagan Faun.

# Spring: Gardens and Flowers

## As White as Milk (Traditional, Riddle, 6+)

As white as milk,
And not milk;
As green as grass,
And not grass;
As red as blood,
And not blood;
As black as soot,
And not soot!

Answer: A bramble-blossom

## Baby Seed Song (Edith Nesbit, Poem, 6+)

Little brown brother, oh! little brown brother,
Are you awake in the dark?
Here we lie cozily, close to each other:
Hark to the song of the lark—
"Waken!" the lark says, "waken and dress you;
Put on your green coats and gay,
Blue sky will shine on you, sunshine caress you—
Waken! 'tis morning—'tis May!"

Little brown brother, oh! little brown brother,
What kind of flower will you be?
I'll be a poppy—all white, like my mother;
Do be a poppy like me.
What! you're a sunflower? How I shall miss you

When you're grown golden and high!
But I shall send all the bees up to kiss you;
Little brown brother, good-bye.

## The City Mouse (Christina Rossetti, Poem, K–5/6+)

The city mouse lives in a house;
The garden mouse lives in a bower,
He's friendly with the frogs and toads,
And sees the pretty plants in flower.
The city mouse eats bread and cheese;
The garden mouse eats what he can;
We will not grudge him seeds and stalks,
Poor little timid furry man.

## Double Dee Double Day (Traditional, Nursery Rhyme, 6+)

Double Dee Double Day,
Set a garden full of seeds;
When the seeds began to grow,
It's like a garden full of snow.
When the snow began to melt,
Like a ship without a belt.
When the ship began to sail,
Like a bird without a tail.
When the bird began to fly,
Like an eagle in the sky.
When the sky began to roar,
Like a Hon* at the door.
When the door began to crack,
Like a stick laid o'er my back.
When my back began to smart,
Like a penknife in my heart.
When my heart began to bleed,
Like a needleful of thread.
When the thread began to rot,
Like a turnip in the pot.
When the pot began to boil,
Like a bottle full of oil.
When the oil began to settle,
Like our Geordies** bloody battle.

*Hon: Another word for Hun, a warring nomadic tribe led by Attila the Hun.
**Geordies: People from Northeast England.

## Draw a Pail of Water (Traditional, Nursery Rhyme, K–5/6+)

Draw a pail of water,
For my lady's daughter;
My father's a king, and my mother's a queen,
My two little sisters are dressed in green,
Stamping grass and parsley,
Marigold leaves and daisies.
One rush! two rush!
Pray thee, fine lady, come under my bush.

## Five Little Flowers (Traditional, Fingerplay, PreS)

Five little flowers standing in the sun (Hold up five fingers.)
See their heads nodding, bowing one by one? (Bend fingers one at a time.)
Down, down, down comes the gentle rain, (Move hands down, wriggling fingers.)
And the five little flowers lift their heads up again! (Show five fingers.)

## Flowers Tall (Traditional, Action Rhyme, PreS)

Flowers tall, flowers small. (Reach arms up, then bend down low.)
Count them one by one.
Blowing with the breezes (Sway arms back and forth.)
In the springtime sun.
1, 2, 3, 4, 5 (Count numbers on fingers.)

## The Green Grass Grew All Around (Traditional, Song, PreS/K–5)

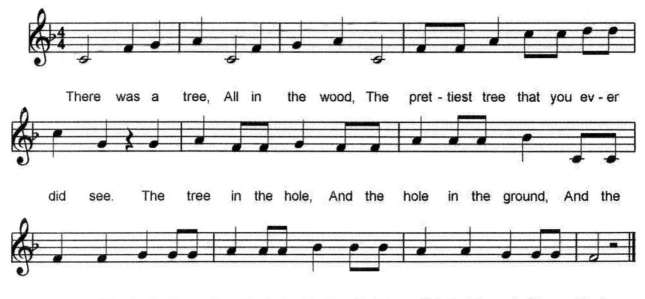

There was a tree, All in the wood, The pret-tiest tree that you ev-er did see. The tree in the hole, And the hole in the ground, And the green grass grew all a-round all a-round and the green grass grew all a-round.

Verse 2: And on that tree,
There was a limb,
The prettiest little limb,
That you ever did see.
The limb on the tree,
And the tree in a hole,
And the hole in the ground.
And the green grass grew
All around, all around,
And the green grass grew all around.
Verse 3: And on that limb, (Repeat.)
There was a branch . . . (Continue same as above.)
Verse 4: And on that branch, (Repeat.)
There was a nest . . .
Verse 5: And in that nest, (Repeat.)
There was an egg . . .
Verse 6: And in that egg, (Repeat.)
There was a bird . . .
Verse 7: And on that bird, (Repeat.)
There was a wing . . .
Verse 8: And on that wing, (Repeat.)
There was a feather . . .

## Here's a Green Leaf (Traditional, Fingerplay, PreS)

Here's a green leaf, (Show one hand.)
And here's a green leaf. (Show another hand.)
That you see makes two. (Show two fingers.)
Here is a bud (Show fist.)
That makes a flower.
Watch it bloom for you. (Push first hand through second hand and open fingers.)

## Hitty Pitty (Traditional, Riddle, K–5/6+)

Hitty Pitty within the wall,
Hitty Pitty without the wall.
If you touch Hitty Pitty,
Hitty Pitty will bite you.

Answer: A nettle

## Hope Is Like a Harebell (Christina Rossetti, Poem, K–5/6+)

Hope is like a harebell trembling from its birth,
Love is like a rose the joy of all the earth;
Faith is like a lily lifted high and white,
Love is like a lovely rose the world's delight;
Harebells and sweet lilies show a thornless growth,
But the rose with all its thorns excels them both.

## I Dug and Dug Amongst the Snow (Christina Rossetti, Poem, K–5/6+)

I dug and dug amongst the snow,
And thought the flowers would never grow;
I dug and dug amongst the sand,
And still no green thing came to hand.
Melt, O snow! the warm winds blow
To thaw the flowers and melt the snow;
But all the winds from every land
Will rear no blossom from the sand.

## I Like to Pretend (Traditional, Action Rhyme, PreS/K–5)

I like to pretend that I am a rose
That grows and grows and grows. (Slowly stand up.)
My hands are a rosebud closed up tight. (Fold hands together.)
With not a tiny speck of light.
Then slowly the petals open for me, (Open hands.)
And now I am a rose, you see. (Bow.)

## In the Garden (Ernest Crosby, Poem, 6+)

I spied beside the garden bed
A tiny lass of ours,
Who stopped and bent her sunny head
Above the red June flowers.

Pushing the leaves and thorns apart,
She singled out a rose,
And in its inmost crimson heart,
Enraptured, plunged her nose.

"O dear, dear rose, come, tell me true—
Come, tell me true," said she,
"If I smell just as sweet to you
As you smell sweet to me!"

## Kind Hearts (Traditional, Nursery Rhyme, K–5/6+)

Kind hearts are the gardens,
Kind thoughts are the roots,
Kind words are the blossoms,
Kind deeds are the fruits;
Love is the sweet sunshine
That warms into life,
For only in darkness
Grow hatred and strife.

## Lady Daffadowndilly (Christina Rossetti, Poem, K–5/6+)

Growing in the vale
By the uplands hilly,
Growing straight and frail,
Lady Daffadowndilly.
In a golden crown,
And a scant green gown
While the spring blows chilly,
Lady Daffadown,
Sweet Daffadowndilly.

## Little Dandelion (Helen Barron Bostwick, Poem, 6+)

Gay little Dandelion
Lights up the meads,
Swings on her slender foot,
Telleth her beads,
Lists to the robin's note
Poured from above;
Wise little Dandelion
Asks not for love.

Cold lie the daisy banks
Clothed but in green,
Where, in the days agone,
Bright hues were seen.

Wild pinks are slumbering,
Violets delay;
True little Dandelion
Greeteth the May.

Brave little Dandelion!
Fast falls the snow,
Bending the daffodil's
Haughty head low.
Under that fleecy tent,
Careless of cold,
Blithe little Dandelion
Counteth her gold.

Meek little Dandelion
Groweth more fair,
Till dies the amber dew
Out from her hair.
High rides the thirsty sun,
Fiercely and high;
Faint little Dandelion
Closeth her eye.

Pale little Dandelion,
In her white shroud,
Heareth the angel-breeze
Call from the cloud;
Tiny plumes fluttering
Make no delay;
Little winged Dandelion
Soareth away.

## The Little Elf (John Kendrick Bangs, Poem, 6+)

I met a little Elf-man, once,
Down where the lilies blow.
I asked him why he was so small,
And why he didn't grow.
He slightly frowned, and with his eye
He looked me through and through.
"I'm quite as big for me," said he,
"As you are big for you."

From *Big Book of Seasons, Holidays, and Weather: Rhymes, Fingerplays, and Songs for Children*
by Elizabeth Cothen Low. Santa Barbara, CA: Libraries Unlimited. Copyright © 2011.

## Little Lad (Traditional, Nursery Rhyme, PreS/K–5)

Little lad, little lad,
Where was thou born?
Far off in Lancashire,*
Under a thorn;
Where they sup sour milk
From a ram's horn.

*Lancashire: An area in Northwest England.

## The Little Plant (Emilie Poulsson, Fingerplay, K–5)

In my little garden bed (Hold ten fingers together to make "garden bed.")
Raked so nicely over, (Perform raking motion on right hand with left hand.)
First the tiny seeds I sow, (Pretend to drop seeds with left hand.)
Then with soft earth cover. (Pretend to cover seeds with left hand.)
Shining down, the great round sun (Raise arms and form circle over head.)
Smiles upon it often;
Little raindrops, pattering down, (Drum with fingertips.)
Help the seeds to soften.

Then the little plant awakes!
Down the roots go creeping. (Point downwards.)
Up it lifts its little head
Through the brown mould peeping.
High and higher still it grows (Elevate the arm and raise the thumb from the hand.)
Through the summer hours,
Till some happy day the buds
Open into flowers. (Open hands.)

## Little White Lily (George Macdonald, Poem, K–5/6+)

Little White Lily sat by a stone,
Drooping and waiting till the sun shone.
Little White Lily sunshine has fed;
Little White Lily is lifting her head.

Little White Lily said: "It is good,
Little White Lily's clothing and food."
Little White Lily dressed like a bride!
Shining with whiteness, and crowned beside!

Little White Lily drooping with pain,
Waiting and waiting for the wet rain,
Little White Lily holdeth her cup;
Rain is fast falling and filling it up.

Little White Lily said: "Good again,
When I am thirsty to have the nice rain.
Now I am stronger, now I am cool;
Heat cannot burn me, my veins are so full."

Little White Lily smells very sweet;
On her head sunshine, rain at her feet.
Thanks to the sunshine, thanks to the rain,
Little White Lily is happy again.

## Marum (Traditional, Riddle, K–5/6+)

If you set it,
The cats will eat it;
If you sow it,
The cats will know it.

Answer: Marum (a plant also known as cat thyme).

## A Man of Words and Not of Deeds (Traditional, Nursery Rhyme, K–5/6+)

A man of words and not of deeds,
Is like a garden full of weeds;
And when the weeds begin to grow,
It's like a garden full of snow;
And when the snow begins to fall,
It's like a bird upon the wall;
And when the bird away does fly,
It's like an eagle in the sky;
And when the sky begins to roar,
It's like a lion at the door;
And when the door begins to crack,
It's like a stick across your back;
And when your back begins to smart,
It's like a penknife in your heart;
And when your heart begins to bleed,
You're dead, and dead, and dead, indeed.

From *Big Book of Seasons, Holidays, and Weather: Rhymes, Fingerplays, and Songs for Children*
by Elizabeth Cothen Low. Santa Barbara, CA: Libraries Unlimited. Copyright © 2011.

## A Man of Words (Traditional, Nursery Rhyme, K–5/6+)

A man of words, and not of deeds,
Is like a garden full of weeds;
For when the weeds begin to grow,
Then doth the garden overflow.

## Mistress Mary (Traditional, Nursery Rhyme, PreS/K–5)

Mistress Mary, quite contrary,
How does your garden grow?
With cockle-shells, and silver bells,
And pretty maids* all in a row.

*Instead of "pretty maids" in the last line, other versions refer to marigolds, columbines, and cowslips.

## Nettles Grow in an Angry Bush (Traditional, Bouncing Rhyme, B/PreS)

Nettles grow in an angry bush,
An angry bush, an angry bush;
Nettles grow in an angry bush,
With my High, Ho, Ham!

This is the way the lady goes,
The lady goes, the lady goes;
This is the way the lady goes,
With my High, Ho, Ham!

## Putting in the Seed (Robert Frost, Poem, 6+)

You come to fetch me from my work to-night
When supper's on the table, and we'll see
If I can leave off burying the white
Soft petals fallen from the apple tree.
(Soft petals, yes, but not so barren quite,
Mingled with these, smooth bean and wrinkled pea;)
And go along with you ere you lose sight
Of what you came for and become like me,
Slave to a springtime passion for the earth.
How Love burns through the Putting in the Seed
On through the watching for that early birth
When, just as the soil tarnishes with weed,
The sturdy seedling with arched body comes
Shouldering its way and shedding the earth crumbs.

## Round and Round the Garden (Traditional, Action Rhyme, B/PreS)

Round and round the garden (Have your fingers go round child's wrist.)
Like a Teddy Bear.
One step, (Have your fingers walk up child's arm.)
Two steps,
Tickly under there. (Tickle child under armpit.)

## This Is My Garden (Traditional, Fingerplay, PreS/K–5)

This is my garden (Hold out left hand, with palm facing upward.
I'll rake it with care, (Perform raking motion on left hand with right hand.)
And then some flower seeds (Pretend to drop seeds on left hand.)
I'll plant in there.
The sun will shine (Raise arms and form circle over head.)
And the rain will fall, (Wriggle fingers and slowly bring them down to lap.)
And my garden will blossom (Push first hand through second hand and open fingers.)
And grow straight and tall.

## This Is the Key of the Kingdom (Traditional, Nursery Rhyme, PreS/K–5)

This is the key of the kingdom.
In that kingdom there is a city.
In that city there is a town.
In that town there is a street.
In that street there is a lane.
In that lane there is a yard.
In that yard there is a house.
In that house there is a room.
In that room there is a bed.
On that bed there is a basket.
In that basket there are some flowers.
Flowers in the basket, basket on the bed,
Bed in the room, room in the house,
House in the yard, yard in the lane,
Lane in the street, street in the town,
Town in the city, city in the kingdom,
Of that kingdom this is the key.

## Thou Pretty Herb of Venus' Tree (Traditional, Nursery Rhyme, K–5/6+)

Thou pretty herb of Venus' tree,
Thy true name it is yarrow;
Now who my bosom friend must be,
Pray tell thou me tomorrow.

## Twist Me a Crown of Wind-Flowers (Christina Rossetti, Poem, K–5/6+)

Twist me a crown of wind-flowers;
That I may fly away
To hear the singers at their song,
And players at their play.
Put on your crown of wind-flowers:
But whither would you go?
Beyond the surging of the seas
And the storms that blow.
Alas! your crown of wind-flowers
Can never make you fly:
I twist them in a crown to-day,
And to-night they die.

## The Violet (Jane Taylor, Poem, K–5/6+)

Down in a green and shady bed
A modest violet grew;
Its stalk was bent, it hung its head,
As if to hide from view.

And yet it was a lovely flower,
Its colors bright and fair;
It might have graced a rosy bower,
Instead of hiding there.

Yet there it was content to bloom,
In modest tints arrayed;
And there diffused a sweet perfume,
Within the silent shade.

Then let me to the valley go,
This pretty flower to see;
That I may also learn to grow
In sweet humility.

## What Do You Suppose? (Traditional, Action Rhyme, PreS/K–5)

What do you suppose?
A bee sat on my nose. (Place right finger on nose.)
Then what do you think?
He gave me a wink (Wink.)
And said, "I beg your pardon,
I thought you were the garden." (Have finger "fly" away from nose.)

## Where Innocent Bright-Eyed Daisies Are (Christina Rossetti, Poem, K–5/6+)

Where innocent bright-eyed daisies are,
With blades of grass between,
Each daisy stands up like a star
Out of a sky of green.

## A White Blossom (D.H. Lawrence, Poem, 6+)

A tiny moon as white and small as a single jasmine flower
Leans all alone above my window, on night's wintry bower,
Liquid as lime-blossom, soft as brilliant water or rain
She shines, the one white love of my youth, which all sin cannot stain.

# Spring Holidays: April Fool's Day

## Pool, Fool (Traditional, Nursery Rhyme, K–5/6+)

Pool, fool, April fool,
You learn nought by going to school!

## April Fool (Traditional, Nursery Rhyme, K–5/6+)

April-fool time's past and gone,
You're the fool, and I'm none!

From *Big Book of Seasons, Holidays, and Weather: Rhymes, Fingerplays, and Songs for Children* by Elizabeth Cothen Low. Santa Barbara, CA: Libraries Unlimited. Copyright © 2011.

# Spring Holidays: Easter

## Care Sunday (Traditional, Nursery Rhyme, PreS/K–5)

Care Sunday.*
Care Sunday, care away,
Palm Sunday and Easter-day.

*Care-Sunday: The Sunday before Palm Sunday, and the two weeks before Easter.

## Easter Bunny's Ears Are Floppy (Traditional, Action Rhyme, B/PreS)

Easter Bunny's ears are floppy. (Bend fingers downward and place on ears.)
Easter Bunny's feet are hoppy. (Touch feet and hop.)
His fur is soft and his nose is fluffy, (Rub arms and nose.)
Tail is short and powder-puffy. (Place fist on lower back for tail.)

## Easter-Gloves (Traditional, Nursery Rhyme, K–5/6+)

Love, to thee I send these gloves,*
If you love me,
Leave out the G,
And make a pair of loves!

*During the sixteenth century, it was customary to make presents of gloves at Easter.

## Five Little Easter Eggs (Traditional, Fingerplay, PreS/K–5)

Five little Easter eggs lovely colors wore; (Show five fingers.)
Mother ate the blue one, then there were four. (Show four fingers.)
Four little Easter eggs, two and two you see;
Daddy ate the red one, then there were three. (Show three fingers.)
Three little Easter eggs, before I knew,
Sister ate the yellow one, then there were two. (Show two fingers.)
Two little Easter eggs, oh, what fun!
Brother ate the purple one, then there was one. (Show one finger.)
One little Easter egg, see me run!
I ate the last one, and then there were none. (Bend down last finger.)

### The Rose Is Red (Traditional, Nursery Rhyme, K–5/6+)

The rose is red, the violet's blue,
The gilly-flower sweet, and so are you;
These are the words you bade me say
For a pair of new gloves on Easter-day.

## Spring Holidays: May Day (First of May)

### Rise Up, Fair Maidens (Traditional, Nursery Rhyme, K–5/6+)

Rise up, fair maidens, fie, for shame,
For I've been four long miles from home;
I've been gathering my garlands gay;
Rise up, fair maids, and take in your May.

### Good Morning, Missus and Master (Traditional, Nursery Rhyme, PreS/K–5)

Good morning, missus and master,
I wish you a happy day;
Please to smell my garland,
'Cause it is the first of May.

### There Is But One May in the Year (Christina Rossetti, Poem, K–5/6+)

There is but one May in the year,
And sometimes May is wet and cold;
There is but one May in the year
Before the year grows old.
Yet though it be the chilliest May,
With least of sun and most of showers,
Its wind and dew, its night and day
Bring up the flowers.

# Spring Weather: Rain/Dew

## The Ants Go Marching (Traditional, Song, PreS/K–5)

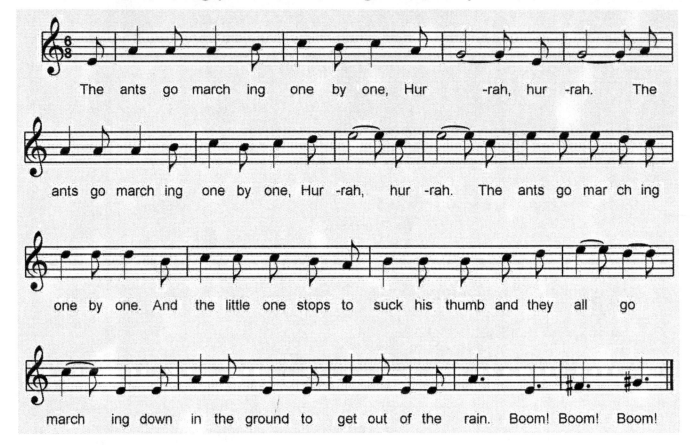

Verse 2: The ants go marching two by two,
Hurrah, hurrah.
The ants go marching two by two,
Hurrah, hurrah.
The ants go marching two by two,
The little one stops to tie his shoe.
And they all go marching down
Into the ground
To get out
Of the rain.
Boom! Boom! Boom!

Verse 3: The ants go marching three by three . . .
The little one stops to climb a tree . . .

Verse 4: The ants go marching four by four . . .
The little one stops to shut the door . . .

Verse 5: The ants go marching five by five . . .
The little one stops to take a dive . . .

Verse 6: The ants go marching six by six . . .
The little one stops to pick up sticks . . .

Verse 7: The ants go marching seven by seven . . .
The little one stops to pray to heaven . . .

Verse 8: The ants go marching eight by eight . . .
The little one stops to shut the gate . . .

Verse 9: The ants go marching nine by nine . . .
The little one stops to check the time . . .

Verse 10: The ants go marching ten by ten,
Hurrah, hurrah.
The ants go marching ten by ten,
Hurrah, hurrah.
The ants go marching ten by ten,
The little one stops to say, "The End!"

## As the Days Grow Longer (Traditional, Nursery Rhyme, K–5/6+)

As the days grow longer,
The storms grow stronger;
As the days lengthen,
So the storms strengthen.

*See also* "Children's Song" (Ford Madox Ford, 6+) in "The Four Seasons" chapter, weather section.

## Doctor Foster (Traditional, Nursery Rhyme, PreS/K–5)

Doctor Foster went to Gloucester,*
In a shower of rain;
He stepped in a puddle up to his middle,
And wouldn't go there again.

*Gloucester: A city in southwest England.

From *Big Book of Seasons, Holidays, and Weather: Rhymes, Fingerplays, and Songs for Children* by Elizabeth Cothen Low. Santa Barbara, CA: Libraries Unlimited. Copyright © 2011.

## The Eentsy, Weentsy Spider (Traditional, Song, Fingerplay, B/PreS)

(Also known as "The Itsy Bitsy Spider," "The Eency Weency Spider," "The Incy Wincy Spider," "The Incey Wincey Spider," and "The Eensy, Weensy Spider.")

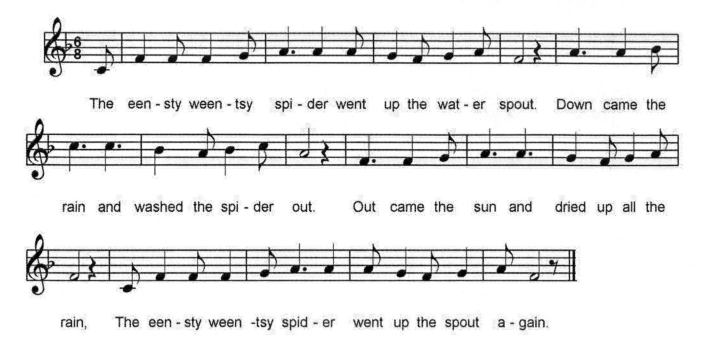

The een-sty ween-tsy spi-der went up the wat-er spout. Down came the rain and washed the spi-der out. Out came the sun and dried up all the rain, The een-sty ween-tsy spid-er went up the spout a-gain.

Verse 1 (Instructions): The eentsy weentsy spider (Place left index finger and right thumb together; then bring right index finger and left thumb together.)
Went up the water spout. (Alternate this pattern moving upward.)
Down came the rain (Wiggle fingers on both hands and move downward.)
And washed the spider out. (Cross hands and then sweep them outward to sides of body.)
Out came the sun (Form circle over head with arms.)
And dried up all the rain;
And the eency weency spider spider (Place left index finger and right thumb together; then bring right index finger and left thumb together.)
Went up the spout again. (Alternate this pattern moving upward.)

## Elf and Dormouse (Oliver Herford, Nursery Rhyme, K–5/6+)

Under a toadstool
Crept a wee Elf,
Out of the rain
To shelter himself
Under the toadstool,
Sound asleep,

Sat a big Dormouse
All in a heap.
Trembled the wee Elf
Frightened, and yet
Fearing to fly away
Lest he get wet.
To the next shelter
Maybe a mile
Sudden the wee Elf
Smiled a wee smile.
Tugged till the toadstool
Toppled in two
Holding it over him
Gaily he flew.
Soon he was safe home,
Dry as could be.
Soon woke the Dormouse
"Good gracious me!
Where is my toadstool!"
Loud he lamented,
And that's how umbrellas
First were invented.

## Evening Red and Morning Gray (Traditional, Saying, K–5/6+)

Evening red and morning gray
Set the traveler on his way,
But evening gray and morning red,
Bring the rain upon his head.

*See also* "If All the Raindrops" (Traditional, Song, PreS/K–5) in "The Four Seasons" chapter, weather section.

## If Bees Stay at Home (Traditional, Saying, PreS/ K–5)

If bees stay at home,
Rain will soon come;
If they fly away,
Fine will be the day.

## It's Raining, It's Pouring (Traditional, Nursery Rhyme, B/PreS/K–5)

It's raining, it's pouring;
The old man is snoring.
He went to bed and he
Bumped his head
And he couldn't get up in the morning.

## The Learned Fish (Hilaire Belloc, Poem, K–5/6+)

This learned Fish has not sufficient brains
To go into the water when it rains.

## Little Raindrops (Traditional, Poem, K–5)

Oh, where do you come from,
You little drops of rain,
Pitter patter, pitter patter,
Down the window-pane?
They won't let me walk,
And they won't let me play,
And they won't let me go
Out of doors at all to-day.
They put away my playthings
Because I broke them all,
And then they locked up all my bricks,
And took away my ball.
Tell me, little raindrops,
Is that the way you play,
Pitter patter, pitter patter,
All the rainy day?
They say I'm very naughty,
But I've nothing else to do
But sit here at the window;
I should like to play with you.
The little raindrops cannot speak,
But "pitter, patter pat"
Means, "We can play on this side:
Why can't you play on that?"

## Over Hill (Shakespeare, from "A Midsummer-Night's Dream," Poem, 6+)

Over hill, over dale,
Through bush, through brier,
Over park, over pale,
Through flood, through fire,
I do wander everywhere,
Swifter than the moon's sphere;
And I serve the fairy queen,
To dew her orbs upon the green:
The cowslips tall her pensioners be;
In their gold coats spots you see;
Those be rubies, fairy favors,
In those freckles live their savors:
I must go seek some dew-drops here,
And hang a pearl in every cowslip's ear.

## Pitter-Patter, Raindrops (Traditional, Fingerplay, PreS/K–5)

Pitter-patter, raindrops,
Falling from the sky; (Wiggle fingers and slowly bring them down to lap.)
Here is my umbrella, (Point right index finger up and place left hand on top, palm facing
    downward.)
To keep me safe and dry!
When the rain is over,
And the sun begins to glow, (Form circle over head with arms.)
Little flowers start to bud,
And grow and grow and grow! (Push first hand through second hand and open fingers.)

## Rain Before Seven (Traditional, Saying, PreS/K–5)

Rain before seven,
Fair by eleven.

## Raindrops, Raindrops! (Traditional, Fingerplay, PreS/K–5)

Raindrops, raindrops,
Falling all around. (Wiggle fingers and slowly bring them down to lap.)
Pitter, patter on the rooftops. (Point up.)
Pitter, patter on the ground. (Point down.)
Here is an umbrella.
It will keep me dry. (Point right index finger up and place left hand on top, palm facing
    downward to form "umbrella.")

From *Big Book of Seasons, Holidays, and Weather: Rhymes, Fingerplays, and Songs for Children*
by Elizabeth Cothen Low. Santa Barbara, CA: Libraries Unlimited. Copyright © 2011.

When I go walking in the rain,
I hold it up so high. (Hold umbrella up high.)

Pitter, patter, raindrops.
Falling from the sky. (Wiggle fingers and slowly bring them down to lap.)
Here is my umbrella, (Point right index finger up and place left hand on top, palm facing
    downward.)
To keep me safe and dry.
When the rain is over,
And the sun begins to glow. (Form circle over head with arms.)
Little flowers start to bud,
And grow and grow and grow! (Push first hand through second hand and open fingers.)

## Rain, Rain, Go to Spain (Traditional, Nursery Rhyme, PreS/K–5)

Rain, rain, go to Spain;
Fair weather, come again.

## Rain, Rain, Go to Spain (Traditional, Nursery Rhyme, PreS/K–5)

Rain, rain, go to Spain;
Come again another day.
When I brew and when I bake,
I'll give you a figgy cake.

## Rain, Rain Go Away (Traditional, Nursery Rhyme, PreS/K–5)

Rain, rain go away,
Come again a Saturday.

## Rain, Rain Go Away (Traditional, Nursery Rhyme, PreS/K–5)

Rain, rain go away,
Come again another day;
Little Johnny wants to play.

*See also* "A Red Sky at Night" (Traditional, Saying, K–5/6+) in "The Four Seasons" chapter, weather section.
*See also* "Round the House" (Traditional, PreS/K–5) in "The Four Seasons" chapter, weather section.
*See also* "Sing, Little Bird" (Traditional, PreS/K–5) in "The Four Seasons" chapter, weather section.

## Slip on Your Raincoat (Traditional, Action Rhyme, PreS/K–5)

Slip on your raincoat, (Mime putting on jacket.)
Pull on your galoshes; (Mime putting on boots.)
Wading in puddles
Makes splishes and sploshes. (Stomp feet and jump into pretend puddles.)

## A Sunshiny Shower (Traditional, Saying, PreS/K–5)

A sunshiny shower
Won't last half an hour.

## A Water There Is I Must Pass (Traditional, Riddle, K–5/6+)

A water there is I must pass,
A broader water never was;
And yet of all waters I ever did see,
To pass over with less jeopardy.

Answer: The dew.

## When Fishes Set Umbrellas Up (Christina Rossetti, Poem, K–5/6+)

When fishes set umbrellas up
If the raindrops run,
Lizards will want their parasols
To shade them from the sun.

## When the Peacock Loudly Calls (Traditional, Saying, K–5/6+)

When the peacock loudly calls,
Then look out for rain and squalls.*

*Squalls: Strong winds.

# Spring Weather: Rainbows

## If All Were Rain and Never Sun (Christina Rosseti, Poem, K–5/6+)

If all were rain and never sun,
No bow could span the hill;
If all were sun and never rain,
There'd be no rainbow still.

*From Big Book of Seasons, Holidays, and Weather: Rhymes, Fingerplays, and Songs for Children*
by Elizabeth Cothen Low. Santa Barbara, CA: Libraries Unlimited. Copyright © 2011.

### If There Be a Rainbow (Traditional, Saying, K–5/6+)

If there be a rainbow in the eve,
It will rain and leave;
But if there be a rainbow in the morrow,
It will neither lend nor borrow.

### Purple, Yellow, Red, and Green (Traditional, Riddle, K–5/6+)

Purple, yellow, red, and green,
The king cannot reach it nor the queen;
Nor can old Noll,* whose power's so great.

Answer: A rainbow.
*Old Noll refers to British military leader Oliver Cromwell.

### Rainbow at Night (Traditional, Saying, K–5/6+)

Rainbow at night
Is the sailor's delight;
Rainbow at morning,
Sailors, take warning.

### Rainbow in the Morning (Traditional, Saying, K–5/6+)

Rainbow in the morning,
Shipper's warning;
Rainbow at night,
Shipper's delight.

## Spring Weather: Wind

### Arthur O' Bower (Traditional, Riddle, K–5/6+)

Arthur O' Bower has broken his band,
He comes roaring up the land,
The King of Scots, with all his power,
Cannot turn Arthur of the Bower.

Answer: A storm of wind/ hurricane.

## Blow the Wind (Traditional, Nursery Rhyme, K–5/6+)

Blow the wind high, blow the wind low,
It bloweth fair to Hawley's hoe.*

*Hawley's Hoe was a group of moorings belonging to a wealthy English merchant in the 1300s.

*See also* "Children's Song" (Ford Madox Ford, 6+) in "The Four Seasons" chapter, weather section.

## Lady Wind (Traditional, Nursery Rhyme, PreS/K–5)

My lady wind, my lady wind, went round about the house
To find a chink to get her foot in, her foot in.
She tried the keyhole in the door,
She tried the crevice in the floor,
And drove the chimney soot in, the soot in.

## Lullaby (Alfred Tennyson, Poem, K–5/6+)

Sweet and low, sweet and low,
Wind of the western sea,
Low, low, breathe and blow,
Wind of the western sea!
Over the rolling waters go,
Come from the dying moon, and blow,
Blow him again to me;
While my little one, while my pretty one, sleeps.

Sleep and rest, sleep and rest,
Father will come to thee soon;
Rest, rest, on mother's breast,
Father will come to thee soon;
Father will come to his babe in the nest,
Silver sails all out of the west
Under the silver moon:
Sleep, my little one, sleep, my pretty one, sleep.

## No Weather Is Ill (Traditional, Saying, K–5/6+)

No weather is ill,
If the wind be still.

From *Big Book of Seasons, Holidays, and Weather: Rhymes, Fingerplays, and Songs for Children* by Elizabeth Cothen Low. Santa Barbara, CA: Libraries Unlimited. Copyright © 2011.

## O Wind, Where Have You Been (Christina Rossetti, Poem, K–5/6+)

O wind, where have you been,
That you blow so sweet?
Among the violets
Which blossom at your feet.
The honeysuckle waits
For Summer and for heat.
But violets in the chilly Spring
Make the turf so sweet.

## O Wind, Why Do You Never Rest (Christina Rossetti, Poem, K–5/6+)

O wind, why do you never rest,
Wandering, whistling to and fro,
Bringing rain out of the west,
From the dim north bringing snow?

## The Road of Remembrance (Lizette Woodworth Reese, Poem, 6+)

The old wind stirs the hawthorn tree;
The tree is blossoming;
Northward the road runs to the sea,
And past the House of Spring.

The folk go down it unafraid;
The still roofs rise before;
When you were lad and I was maid,
Wide open stood the door.

Now, other children crowd the stair,
And hunt from room to room;
Outside, under the hawthorn fair,
We pluck the thorny bloom.

Out in the quiet road we stand,
Shut in from wharf and mart,
The old wind blowing up the land,
The old thoughts at our heart.

## The Piper on the Hill (Dora Sigerson Shorter, Poem, K–5/6+)

There sits a piper on the hill
Who pipes the livelong day,
And when he pipes both loud and shrill,
The frightened people say:
"The wind, the wind is blowing up
'Tis rising to a gale."
The women hurry to the shore
To watch some distant sail.
The wind, the wind, the wind, the wind,
Is blowing to a gale.

But when he pipes all sweet and low,
The piper on the hill,
I hear the merry women go
With laughter, loud and shrill:
"The wind, the wind is coming south
'Twill blow a gentle day."
They gather on the meadow-land
To toss the yellow hay.
The wind, the wind, the wind, the wind,
Is blowing south to-day.

And in the morn, when winter comes,
To keep the piper warm,
The little Angels shake their wings
To make a feather storm:
"The snow, the snow has come at last!"
The happy children call,
And "ring around" they dance in glee,
And watch the snowflakes fall.
The wind, the wind, the wind, the wind,
Has spread a snowy pall.

But when at night the piper plays,
I have not any fear,
Because God's windows open wide
The pretty tune to hear;
And when each crowding spirit looks
From its star window-pane,
A watching mother may behold
Her little child again.
The wind, the wind, the wind, the wind,
May blow her home again.

From *Big Book of Seasons, Holidays, and Weather: Rhymes, Fingerplays, and Songs for Children*
by Elizabeth Cothen Low. Santa Barbara, CA: Libraries Unlimited. Copyright © 2011.

## Rockabye, Baby (Traditional, Song, B/PreS)

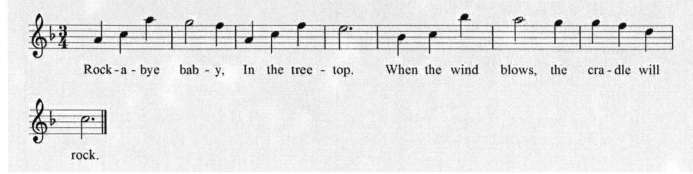

Rock-a-bye bab-y, In the tree-top. When the wind blows, the cra-dle will

rock.

Stanza 2: When the bough breaks, the cradle will fall,
And down will come Baby, cradle and all.


## The South Wind Brings Wet Weather (Traditional, Saying, PreS/K–5/6+)

The south wind brings wet weather,
The north wind wet and cold together;
The west wind always brings us rain,
The east wind blows it back again.


## Voice of the Western Wind (Edmund Clarence Stedman, Poem, 6+)

Voice of the western wind!
Thou singest from afar,
Rich with the music of a land
Where all my memories are;
But in thy song I only hear
The echo of a tone
That fell divinely on my ear
In days forever flown.

Star of the western sky!
Thou beamest from afar,
With lustre caught from eyes I knew
Whose orbs were each a star;
But, oh, those orbs—too wildly bright—
No more eclipse thine own,
And never shall I find the light
Of days forever flown!

## The Wind and the Moon (George Macdonald, Poem, K–5/6+)

Said the Wind to the Moon, "I will blow you out;
You stare
In the air
Like a ghost in a chair,
Always looking what I am about—
I hate to be watched; I'll blow you out."

The Wind blew hard, and out went the Moon.
So, deep
On a heap
Of clouds to sleep,
Down lay the Wind, and slumbered soon,
Muttering low, "I've done for that Moon."

He turned in his bed; she was there again!
On high
In the sky,
With her one ghost eye,
The Moon shone white and alive and plain.
Said the Wind, "I will blow you out again."

The Wind blew hard, and the Moon grew dim.
"With my sledge,
And my wedge,
I have knocked off her edge!
If only I blow right fierce and grim,
The creature will soon be dimmer than dim."

He blew and he blew, and she thinned to a thread.
"One puff
More's enough
To blow her to snuff!
One good puff more where the last was bred,
And glimmer, glimmer, glum will go the thread."

He blew a great blast, and the thread was gone.
In the air
Nowhere
Was a moonbeam bare;
Far off and harmless the shy stars shone—
Sure and certain the Moon was gone!

From *Big Book of Seasons, Holidays, and Weather: Rhymes, Fingerplays, and Songs for Children*
by Elizabeth Cothen Low. Santa Barbara, CA: Libraries Unlimited. Copyright © 2011.

The Wind he took to his revels once more;
On down,
In town,
Like a merry-mad clown,
He leaped and halloed with whistle and roar—
"What's that?" The glimmering thread once more!

He flew in a rage—he danced and blew;
But in vain
Was the pain
Of his bursting brain;
For still the broader the Moon-scrap grew,
The broader he swelled his big cheeks and blew.

Slowly she grew—till she filled the night,
And shone
On her throne
In the sky alone,
A matchless, wonderful silvery light,
Radiant and lovely, the queen of the night.

Said the Wind: "What a marvel of power am I!
With my breath,
Good faith!
I blew her to death—
First blew her away right out of the sky—
Then blew her in; what strength have I!"

But the Moon she knew nothing about the affair;
For high
In the sky,
With her one white eye,
Motionless, miles above the air,
She had never heard the great Wind blare.

## The Wind Blows East (Henry W. Longfellow, Poem, PreS/K–5/6+)

The wind blows east,
The wind blows west,
The blue eggs in robin's nest
Will soon have wings
And flutter and fly away.

## Wind Came Out to Play (Traditional, Nursery Rhyme, PreS/K–5)

The wind came out to play one day.
He swept the clouds out of his way.
He blew the leaves and away they flew.
The trees bent low, and their branches did, too!
The wind blew the great big ships at sea.
The wind blew my kite away from me!

## The Wind's Song (Gabriel Setoun, Poem, K–5/6+)

O winds that blow across the sea,
What is the story that you bring?
Leaves clap their hands on every tree
And birds about their branches sing.

You sing to flowers and trees and birds
Your sea-songs over all the land.
Could you not stay and whisper words
A little child might understand?

The roses nod to hear you sing;
But though I listen all the day,
You never tell me anything
Of father's ship so far away.

Its masts are taller than the trees;
Its sails are silver in the sun;
There's not a ship upon the seas
So beautiful as father's one.

With wings spread out it flies so fast
It leaves the waves all white with foam.
Just whisper to me, blowing past,
If you have seen it sailing home.

I feel your breath upon my cheek,
And in my hair, and on my brow.
Dear winds, if you could only speak,
I know that you would tell me now.

My father's coming home, you'd say,
With precious presents, one, two, three;
A shawl for mother, beads for May,
And eggs and shells for Rob and me.

The winds sing songs where'er they roam;
The leaves all clap their little hands;
For father's ship is coming home
With wondrous things from foreign lands.

## Windy Nights (Robert Louis Stevenson, Poem, K–5/6+)

Whenever the moon and stars are set,
Whenever the wind is high,
All night long in the dark and wet,
A man goes riding by.
Late in the night when the fires are out,
Why does he gallop and gallop about?

Whenever the trees are crying aloud,
And ships are tossed at sea,
By, on the highway, low and loud,
By at the gallop goes he.
By at the gallop he goes, and then
By he comes back at the gallop again.

## When the Wind Is in the East (Traditional, Saying, K–5/6+)

When the wind is in the east,
'Tis good for neither man nor beast;
When the wind is in the north,
The skillful fisher goes not forth;
When the wind is in the south,
It blows the bait in the fishes' mouth;
When the wind is in the west,
Then it is at its very best.

## When the Wind Is in the East (Traditional, Saying, K–5/6+)

When the wind is in the east,
'Tis neither good for man nor beast:
When the wind is in the south,
It is in the rain's mouth.

## When the Wind Is the East (Traditional, Saying, K–5/6+)

When the wind is in the east,
Then the fishes do bite least;
When the wind is in the west,
Then the fishes bite the best;
When the wind is in the north,
Then the fishes do come forth;
When the wind is in the south,
It blows the bait in the fish's mouth.

## Who Has Seen the Wind (Christina Rossetti, Poem, K–5/6+)

Who has seen the wind?
Neither I nor you:
But when the leaves hang trembling,
The wind is passing through.

Who has seen the wind?
Neither you nor I:
But when the trees bow down their heads,
The wind is passing by.

# Summer

The entries in this section are about summer and related subjects, such as sunny weather.

## As I Was Going to Banbury (Traditional, Nursery Rhyme, K–5/6+)

As I was going to Banbury,*
Upon a summer's day,
My dame had butter, eggs, and fruit,
And I had corn and hay.
Joe drove the ox, and Tom the swine,
Dick took the foal and mare.
I sold them all—then home to dine,
From famous Banbury fair.

*Banbury: A town near London.

## Bobbin-a-Bobbin (Traditional, Nursery Rhyme, K–5/6+)

Bobbin-a-Bobbin bent his bow,
And shot at a woodcock and killed a yowe.*
The yowe cried ba, and he ran away,
But never came back till midsummer day.

*Yowe: A ewe.

*See also* "Cuckoo, Cuckoo" (Traditional, PreS/K–5) in "The Four Seasons" chapter.
*See also* "The Cuckoo Comes in April" (Traditional, PreS/K–5) in "The Four Seasons" chapter.
*See also* "The Fairybook" (Norman Gale, K–5/6+) in "The Four Seasons" chapter.

## The Fairies of the Caldon-Low: A Midsummer Legend (Mary Howitt, Poem, 6+)

"And where have you been, my Mary,
And where have you been from me?"
"I've been to the top of the Caldon-Low,*
The midsummer night to see!"

"And what did you see, my Mary,
All up on the Caldon-Low?"
"I saw the glad sunshine come down,
And I saw the merry winds blow."

"And what did you hear, my Mary,
All up on the Caldon-Hill?"
"I heard the drops of the water made,
And the ears of the green corn fill."

"Oh, tell me all, my Mary—
All—all that ever you know;
For you must have seen the fairies
Last night on the Caldon-Low!"

"Then take me on your knee, mother,
And listen, mother of mine:
A hundred fairies danced last night,
And the harpers they were nine.

"And their harp-strings rang so merrily
To their dancing feet so small;
But, oh! the words of their talking
Were merrier far than all!"

"And what were the words, my Mary,
That you did hear them say?"
"I'll tell you all, my mother,
But let me have my way.

"Some of them played with the water,
And rolled it down the hill;
'And this,' they said, 'shall speedily turn
The poor old miller's mill.

" 'For there has been no water
Ever since the first of May;
And a busy man will the miller be
At the dawning of the day!

" 'Oh! the miller, how he will laugh,
When he sees the mill-dam rise!
The jolly old miller, how he will laugh,
Till the tears fill both his eyes!'

"And some they seized the little winds,
That sounded over the hill,
And each put a horn into his mouth,
And blew both loud and shrill:

" 'And there,' said they, 'the merry winds go
Away from every horn;
And they shall clear the mildew dank
From the blind old widow's corn.

" 'Oh, the poor blind widow—
Though she has been blind so long,
She'll be merry enough when the mildew's gone,
And the corn stands tall and strong!'

"And some they brought the brown linseed
And flung it down the Low:
'And this,' said they, 'by the sunrise
In the weaver's croft shall grow!

" 'Oh, the poor lame weaver!
How will he laugh outright
When he sees his dwindling flax-field
All full of flowers by night!'

"And then outspoke a brownie,
With a long beard on his chin:
'I have spun up all the tow,' said he,
'And I want some more to spin.

" 'I've spun a piece of hempen cloth
And I want to spin another—
A little sheet for Mary's bed,
And an apron for her mother!'

"With that I could not help but laugh,
And I laughed out loud and free;
And then on the top of the Caldon-Low
There was no one left but me.

"And all on the top of the Caldon-Low
The mists were cold and gray,
And nothing I saw but the mossy stones
That round about me lay.

"But, coming down from the hill-top,
I heard, afar below,
How busy the jolly miller was,
And how merry the wheel did go!

"And I peeped into the widow's field,
And, sure enough, was seen
The yellow ears of the mildewed corn
All standing stout and green.

"And down the weaver's croft I stole,
To see if the flax were sprung;
And I met the weaver at his gate
With the good news on his tongue!

"Now, this is all I heard, mother,
And all that I did see;
So, prithee, make my bed, mother,
For I'm tired as I can be!"

*Caldon-Low: A group of limestone quarries at Caldon Low in the Staffordshire Moorlands in England.

*See also* "The Garden Year" (Sara Coleridge, K–5/6+) in "The Four Seasons" chapter.

## Grasshopper Green (Traditional, Poem, K–5/6+)

Grasshopper Green is a comical chap;
He lives on the best of fare.
Bright little trousers, jacket, and cap,
These are his summer wear.
Out in the meadow he loves to go,
Playing away in the sun;
Its hopperty, skipperty, high and low—
Summer's the time for fun.

Grasshopper Green has a dozen wee boys,
And soon as their legs grow strong,
Each of them joins in his frolicsome joys,
Singing his merry song.
Under the hedge in a happy row
Soon as the day has begun
Its hopperty, skipperty, high and low—
Summer's the time for fun.

Grasshopper Green has a quaint little house.
It's under the hedge so gay.
Grandmother Spider, as still as a mouse,
Watches him over the way.
Gladly he's calling the children, I know,
Out in the beautiful sun;
It's hopperty, skipperty, high and low—
Summer's the time for fun.

*See also* "The Human Seasons" (John Keats, 6+) in "The Four Seasons" chapter.

## In July (Traditional, Saying, 6+)

In July
Some reap rye.
In August,
If one won't, the other must.

*See also* "January Cold Desolate" (Christina Rossetti, K–5/6+) in "The Four Seasons" chapter.
*See also* "Lazy Lawrence" (Traditional, PreS/K–5) in "The Four Seasons" chapter.

## A Little Boy's Walk (Emilie Poulsson, Fingerplay, PreS/K–5)

A little boy went walking
One lovely summer's day.
He saw a little rabbit (Hold up index and middle finger in a "V" shape.)
That quickly ran away; (Hide hand behind hand.)
He saw a shining river go winding in and out,
And little fishes in it (Place palms together and bend wrists back and forth.)
Were swimming all about;
And slowly, slowly turning,
The great wheel of the mill; (Make two fists and roll them around one another.)
And then the tall church steeple,
The little church so still; (Interlock all fingers, except index fingers, which stand up straight.)
The bridge above the water. (Interlock fingers and point thumbs downward.)
And when he stopped to rest,
He saw among the bushes a wee ground-sparrow's nest. (Cup hands together.)
And as he watched the birdies (Link thumbs together and wiggle fingers above head.)
Above the tree-tops fly,
He saw the clouds a-sailing (Look up and point at the ceiling.)
Across the sunny sky.
He saw the insects playing; (Wiggle fingers on the ground.)
The flowers that summer brings; (Open hands wide.)
He said, "I'll go tell mamma!
I've seen so many things!"

## My Dear, Do You Know (Traditional, Poem, K–5/6+)

My dear, do you know
How a long time ago,
Two poor little children,
Whose names I don't know,
Were stolen away on a fine summer's day,
And left in a wood, as I've heard people say.
And when it was night,
So sad was their plight,
The sun it went down,
And the moon gave no light!
They sobbed and they sighed,
And they bitterly cried,
And the poor little things,
They laid down and died.
And when they were dead,
The robins so red
Brought strawberry leaves,

And over them spread;
And all the day long,
They sang them this song—
"Poor babes in the wood!
Poor babes in the wood!
And don't you remember
The babes in the wood?"

## The Oven Bird (Robert Frost, Poem, 6+)

There is a singer everyone has heard,
Loud, a mid-summer and a mid-wood bird,
Who makes the solid tree trunks sound again.
He says that leaves are old and that for flowers
Mid-summer is to spring as one to ten.
He says the early petal-fall is past
When pear and cherry bloom went down in showers
On sunny days a moment overcast;
And comes that other fall we name the fall.
He says the highway dust is over all.
The bird would cease and be as other birds
But that he knows in singing not to sing.
The question that he frames in all but words
Is what to make of a diminished thing.

## Rushes in a Watery Place (Christina Rossetti, Poem, K–5/6+)

Rushes in a watery place,
And reeds in a hollow;
A soaring skylark in the sky,
A darting swallow;
And where pale blossom used to hang
Ripe fruit to follow.

## The Summer Nights Are Short (Christina Rossetti, Poem, K–5/6+)

The summer nights are short
Where northern days are long:
For hours and hours lark after lark
Trills out his song.
The summer days are short
Where southern nights are long:

Yet short the night when nightingales
Trill out their song.

*See also* "The Seasons" (Traditional, K–5/ 6+) in "The Four Seasons"chapter.
*See also* "A Swarm of Bees in May" (Traditional, K–5/6+) in "The Four Seasons" chapter.
*See also* "Thirty Days Hath September" (Traditional, K–5, 6+) in "The Four Seasons" chapter.

## When a Mounting Skylark Sings (Christina Rossetti, Poem, K–5/6+)

When a mounting skylark sings
In the sunlit summer morn,
I know that heaven is up on high,
And on earth are fields of corn.
But when a nightingale sings
In the moonlit summer even,
I know not if earth is merely earth,
Only that heaven is heaven.

## Where the Bee Sucks (from "The Tempest" by Shakespeare, Poem, 6+)

Where the bee sucks, there suck I:
In a cowslip's bell I lie;
There I couch when owls do cry.
On the bat's back I do fly
After summer merrily:
Merrily, merrily, shall I live now,
Under the blossom that hangs on the bough.

# Summer Weather: Sunshine

*See also* "Children's Song" (Ford Madox Ford, 6+) in "The Four Seasons" chapter, weather section
*See also* "The Evening Red" (Traditional, K–5/6+) in "The Four Seasons" chapter, weather section.

## Five Little Busy Bees (Traditional, Fingerplay, PreS/K–5)

Five little busy bees on a day so sunny, (Hold up five fingers.)
Number one said, "I'd like to make some honey." (Bend first finger.)
Number two said, "Tell me, where shall it be?" (Bend second finger.)
Number three said, "In the old honey tree." (Bend third finger.)
Number four said, "Let's gather pollen sweet." (Bend fourth finger.)
Number five said,"Let's take it on our feet." (Bend fifth finger.)
Humming their busy little honey bee song.
Buzzz . . ..

## A Frisky Lamb (Christina Rossetti, Poem, PreS/K–5)

A frisky lamb
And a frisky child
Playing their pranks
In a cowslip meadow:
The sky all blue
And the air all mild
And the fields all sun
And the lanes half shadow.

## God's Care (Traditional, Nursery Rhyme, PreS/K–5)

In the pleasant sunny meadows,
Where the buttercups are seen,
And the daisies' little shadows
Lie along the level green,
Flocks of quiet sheep are feeding,
Little lambs are playing near,
And the watchful shepherd leading
Keeps them safe from harm and fear.
Like the lambs we little children
Have a shepherd kind and good;
It is God who watches o'er us,
Gives us life and daily food.

## Glad Day (W. Graham Robertson, Poem, 6+)

Here's another day, dear,
Here's the sun again
Peeping in his pleasant way
Through the window pane.
Rise and let him in, dear,
Hail him "hip hurray!"
Now the fun will all begin.
Here's another day!

Down the coppice path,* dear,
Through the dewy glade,
(When the Morning took her bath
What a splash she made!)
Up the wet wood-way, dear,
Under dripping green
Run to meet another day,
Brightest ever seen.

Mushrooms in the field, dear,
Show their silver gleam.
What a dainty crop they yield
Firm as clouted cream,
Cool as balls of snow, dear,
Sweet and fresh and round!
Ere the early dew can go
We must clear the ground.

Such a lot to do, dear,
Such a lot to see!
How we ever can get through
Fairly puzzles me.
Hurry up and out, dear,
Then—away! away!
In and out and round about,
Here's another day!

*Coppice path: A path between hedges or thickets.

## Hick-a-More (Traditional, Riddle, K–5/6+)

Hick-a-more, Hack-a-more,
Hung on a kitchen-door;
Nothing so long,
And nothing so strong,
As Hick-a-more Hack-a-more,
Hung on the kitchen-door!

Answer: A sunbeam.

## Home on the Range (Brewster M. Higley, Song, K–5/6+)

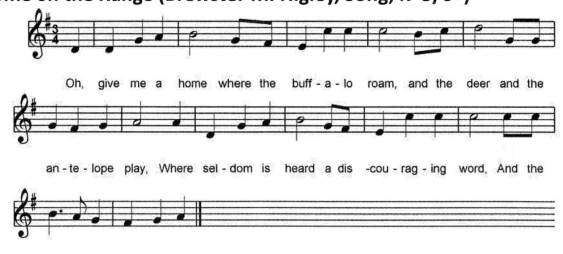

Oh, give me a home where the buff-a-lo roam, and the deer and the

an-te-lope play, Where sel-dom is heard a dis-cou-rag-ing word, And the

sky is not cloudy all day.

Chorus:

Home, Home on the range, where the deer and the an-te-lope play. Where seldom is heard a dis-cou-rag-ing word, And the sky is not cloud-y all day.

Verse 2: How often at night when the heavens are bright
With the light of the glittering stars,
Have I stood there amazed and asked as I gazed,
If their glory exceeds that of ours.

*See also* "If All the Raindrops" (Traditional, PreS/K–5) in "The Four Seasons" chapter, weather section.

## Mister Sun (Traditional, Song, B/PreS/K–5)

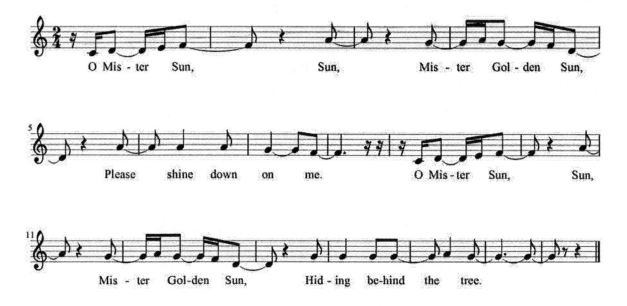

O Mis-ter Sun, Sun, Mis-ter Gol-den Sun, Please shine down on me. O Mis-ter Sun, Sun, Mis-ter Gol-den Sun, Hid-ing be-hind the tree.

Verse 2: These little children
are asking you.
To please come out
so we can play with you.

Oh Mister Sun, Sun,
Mister Golden Sun.
Won't you please shine down on me?

*See also* "Sing, Little Bird" (Traditional, PreS/K–5) in "The Four Seasons" chapter, weather section.

## Sir Lark and King Sun: A Parable (George Macdonald, Poem, 6+)

"Good morrow, my lord!" in the sky alone,
Sang the lark, as the sun ascended his throne.
"Shine on me, my lord; I only am come,
Of all your servants, to welcome you home.
I have flown right up, a whole hour, I swear,
To catch the first shine of your golden hair."

"Must I thank you, then," said the king, "Sir Lark,
For flying so high and hating the dark?
You ask a full cup for half a thirst:
Half was love of me, and half love to be first.
There's many a bird makes no such haste,
But waits till I come: that's as much to my taste."

And King Sun hid his head in a turban of cloud,
And Sir Lark stopped singing, quite vexed and cowed;
But he flew up higher, and thought, "Anon
The wrath of the king will be over and gone;
And his crown, shining out of its cloudy fold,
Will change my brown feathers to a glory of gold."

So he flew—with the strength of a lark he flew;
But, as he rose, the cloud rose too;
And not one gleam of the golden hair
Came through the depths of the misty air;
Till, weary with flying, with sighing sore,
The strong sun-seeker could do no more.

His wings had had no chrism* of gold:
And his feathers felt withered and worn and old;

He faltered, and sank, and dropped like a stone.
And there on her nest, where he left her, alone
Sat his little wife on her little eggs,
Keeping them warm with wings and legs.

Did I say alone? Ah, no such thing!
Full in her face was shining the king.
"Welcome, Sir Lark! You look tired," said he;
"Up is not always the best way to me.
While you have been singing so high and away,
I've been shining to your little wife all day."

He had set his crown all about the nest,
And out of the midst shone her little brown breast;
And so glorious was she in russet gold,
That for wonder and awe Sir Lark grew cold.
He popped his head under her wing, and lay
As still as a stone, till King Sun was away.

*Chrism: Holy consecrated or holy oil.

# Autumn

The entries in this section are about autumn and related subjects, such as harvest and cloudy weather. Holidays occurring during the fall are also included.

## Fly Away, Fly Away Over the Sea (Christina Rossetti, Poem, PreS/K–5/6+)

Fly away, fly away over the sea,
Sun-loving swallow, for summer is done;
Come again, come again, come back to me,
Bringing the summer and bringing the sun.

*See also* "The Garden Year" (Sara Coleridge, K–5/6+) in "The Four Seasons" chapter.
*See also* "The Human Seasons" (John Keats, 6+) in "The Four Seasons" chapter.
*See also* "January Cold Desolate" (Christina Rossetti, K–5/6+) in "The Four Seasons" chapter.

## The Little Maiden and the Little Bird (Lydia Maria Child, Poem, K–5/6+)

"Little bird! little bird! come to me!
I have a green cage ready for thee—
Beauty bright flowers I'll bring thee anew,
And fresh, ripe cherries, all wet with dew."
"Thanks, little maiden, for all thy care,—
But I love dearly the clear, cool air,
And my snug little nest in the old oak tree."

"Little bird! little bird! stay with me!"
"Nay, little damsel! away I'll fly
To greener fields and warmer sky;
When spring returns with pattering rain,
You'll hear my merry song again."

"Little bird! little bird! who'll guide thee
Over the hills and over the sea?
Foolish one! come in the house to stay,
For I'm very sure you'll lose your way."
"Ah, no, little maiden! God guides me
Over the hills and over the sea;
I will be free as the rushing air
And sing of sunshine everywhere."

*See also* "On the First of March" (Traditional, K–5/ 6+) in "The Four Seasons" chapter.
*See also* "The Seasons" (Traditional, K–5/ 6+) in "The Four Seasons" chapter.

## Swallow, Swallow (Traditional, Nursery Rhyme, PreS/K–5)

Swallow, Swallow, neighbor Swallow,
Starting on your autumn flight,
Pause a moment at my window,
Twitter softly a good night.
Now the summer days are ended,
All your duties are well done,
And the little homes you've builded
Have grown empty, one by one.

Swallow, Swallow, neighbor Swallow,
Are you ready for your flight?
Are the little coats completed?
Are the feathered caps all right?
Are the young wings strong and steady
For their flight to warmer sky?
Come again in early springtime.
Until then, good-by, good-by.

*See also* "Thirty Days Hath September" (Traditional, K–5/6+) in "The Four Seasons" chapter.

## To Autumn (John Keats, Poem, 6+)

I. Season of mists and mellow fruitfulness,
Close bosom-friend of the maturing sun;

Conspiring with him how to load and bless
With fruit the vines that round the thatch-eaves run;
To bend with apples the moss'd cottage-trees,
And fill all fruit with ripeness to the core;
To swell the gourd, and plump the hazel shells
With a sweet kernel; to set budding more,
And still more, later flowers for the bees,
Until they think warm days will never cease,
For summer has o'er-brimm'd their clammy cells.

II. Who hath not seen thee oft amid thy store?
Sometimes whoever seeks abroad may find
Thee sitting careless on a granary floor,
Thy hair soft-lifted by the winnowing wind;
Or on a half-reap'd furrow sound asleep,
Drows'd with the fume of poppies, while thy hook
Spares the next swath and all its twined flowers:
And sometimes like a gleaner thou dost keep
Steady thy laden head across a brook;
Or by a cyder-press, with patient look,
Thou watchest the last oozings hours by hours.

III. Where are the songs of spring? Ay, where are they?
Think not of them, thou hast thy music too,—
While barred clouds bloom the soft-dying day,
And touch the stubble-plains with rosy hue;
Then in a wailful choir the small gnats mourn
Among the river sallows, borne aloft
Or sinking as the light wind lives or dies;
And full-grown lambs loud bleat from hilly bourn;
Hedge-crickets sing; and now with treble soft
The red-breast whistles from a garden-croft;
And gathering swallows twitter in the skies.

# Autumn: Foliage

## Here Is an Oak Tree (Traditional, Action Rhyme, PreS/K–5)

Here is an oak tree, straight and tall (Stand up.)
And here are its branches wide. (Stretch out arms and legs.)
Here is a nest of twigs and moss (Cup left hand.)
With three little birds inside. (Show three right-hand fingers perched on left hand.)

From *Big Book of Seasons, Holidays, and Weather: Rhymes, Fingerplays, and Songs for Children*
by Elizabeth Cothen Low. Santa Barbara, CA: Libraries Unlimited. Copyright © 2011.

## How the Leaves Came Down (Susan Coolidge, Poem, K–5/6+)

I'll tell you how the leaves came down.
The great Tree to his children said:
"You're getting sleepy, Yellow and Brown,
Yes, very sleepy, little Red.
It is quite time to go to bed."

"Ah!" begged each silly, pouting leaf,
"Let us a little longer stay;
Dear Father Tree, behold our grief!
'Tis such a very pleasant day,
We do not want to go away."

So, just for one more merry day
To the great Tree the leaflets clung,
Frolicked and danced, and had their way,
Upon the autumn breezes swung,
Whispering all their sports among—

"Perhaps the great Tree will forget,
And let us stay until the spring,
If we all beg, and coax, and fret."
But the great Tree did no such thing;
He smiled to hear them whispering.

"Come, children, all to bed," he cried;
And ere the leaves could urge their prayer,
He shook his head, and far and wide,
Fluttering and rustling everywhere,
Down sped the leaflets through the air.

I saw them; on the ground they lay,
Golden and red, a huddled swarm,
Waiting till one from far away,
White bedclothes heaped upon her arm,
Should come to wrap them safe and warm.

The great bare Tree looked down and smiled.
"Goodnight dear little leaves," he said.
And from below each sleepy child
Replied, "Goodnight," and murmured,
"It is so nice to go to bed!"

## Late Leaves (Walter Savage Landor, Poem, 6+)

The leaves are falling; so am I;
The few late flowers have moisture in the eye;
So have I too.
Scarcely on any bough is heard
Joyous, or even unjoyous, bird
The whole wood through.

Winter may come: he brings but nigher
His circle (yearly narrowing) to the fire
Where old friends meet.
Let him; now heaven is overcast,
And spring and summer both are past,
And all things sweet.

## Leaves Are Floating (Traditional, Fingerplay, PreS/K–5)

Leaves are floating softly down. (Wiggle fingers toward lap.)
They make a carpet on the ground. (Touch ground.)
Then whoosh, the wind comes whistling by, (Move hands from left to right.)
And sends them dancing to the sky. (Wiggle fingers up high.)

## Little Leaves Fall Gently Down (Traditional, Fingerplay, PreS/K–5)

Little leaves fall gently down, (Wiggle fingers toward lap.)
Red and yellow, orange and brown,
Whirling, whirling, round and round, (Move hands in a circular motion.)
Quietly, without a sound,
Falling softly to the ground, (Slowly move hands toward ground.)
Down—and—down—and—down—and down!

## October's Party (George Cooper, Poem, K–5/6+)

October gave a party;
The leaves by hundreds came—
The Chestnuts, Oaks, and Maples,
And leaves of every name.
The Sunshine spread a carpet,
And everything was grand,
Miss Weather led the dancing,
Professor Wind the band.

The Chestnuts came in yellow,
The Oaks in crimson dressed;
The lovely Misses Maple
In scarlet looked their best;
All balanced to their partners,
And gaily fluttered by;
The sight was like a rainbow
New fallen from the sky.

Then, in the rustic hollow,
At hide-and-seek they played,
The party closed at sundown,
And everybody stayed.
Professor Wind played louder;
They flew along the ground;
And then the party ended
In jolly "hands around."

## Autumn: Harvest

### After Apple-Picking (Robert Frost, Poem, 6+)

My long two-pointed ladder's sticking through a tree
Toward heaven still,
And there's a barrel that I didn't fill
Beside it, and there may be two or three
Apples I didn't pick upon some bough.
But I am done with apple-picking now.
Essence of winter sleep is on the night,
The scent of apples: I am drowsing off.
I cannot rub the strangeness from my sight
I got from looking through a pane of glass
I skimmed this morning from the drinking trough
And held against the world of hoary grass.
It melted, and I let it fall and break.
But I was well
Upon my way to sleep before it fell,
And I could tell
What form my dreaming was about to take.
Magnified apples appear and disappear,

Stem end and blossom end,
And every fleck of russet showing clear.
My instep arch not only keeps the ache,
It keeps the pressure of a ladder-round.
I feel the ladder sway as the boughs bend.
And I keep hearing from the cellar bin
The rumbling sound
Of load on load of apples coming in.
For I have had too much
Of apple-picking: I am overtired
Of the great harvest I myself desired.
There were ten thousand thousand fruit to touch,
Cherish in hand, lift down, and not let fall.
For all
That struck the earth,
No matter if not bruised or spiked with stubble,
Went surely to the cider-apple heap
As of no worth.
One can see what will trouble
This sleep of mine, whatever sleep it is.
Were he not gone,
The woodchuck could say whether it's like his
Long sleep, as I describe its coming on,
Or just some human sleep.

## As I Went Through the Garden Gap (Traditional, Riddle, K–5/6+)

As I went through the garden gap,
Who should I meet but Dick Red-cap!
A stick in his hand, a stone in his throat,
If you'll tell me this riddle, I'll give you a groat.

Answer: A cherry.

## At the End of My Yard (Traditional, Riddle, 6+)

At the end of my yard there is a vat,
Four-and-twenty ladies dancing in that:
Some in green gowns, and some with blue hat:
He is a wise man who can tell me that.

Answer: A field of flax.

## The Barley Mow (Traditional, Nursery Rhyme, 6+)

Here's a health to the barley mow,
Here's a health to the man,
Who very well can
Both harrow, and plough, and sow.
When it is well sown,
See it is well mown,
Both raked and graveled clean,
And a barn to lay it in:
Here's a health to the man,
Who very well can
Both thrash and fan it clean.

## Catch Him, Crow (Traditional, Nursery Rhyme, PreS/K–5)

Catch him, crow! Carry him, kite!
Take him away 'til the apples are ripe;
When they are ripe and ready to fall,
Here comes Johnny, apples, and all.

## Cherries (Traditional, Nursery Rhyme, K–5/6+)

Under the trees, the farmer said,
Smiling and shaking his wise old head:
"Cherries are ripe! but then, you know,
There's the grass to cut and the corn to hoe;
We can gather the cherries any day,
But when the sun shines we must make our hay;
To-night, when the work has all been done,
We'll muster the boys, for fruit and fun."

Up on the tree a robin said, Perking and cocking his saucy head,
"Cherries are ripe! and so to-day
We'll gather them while you make the hay;
For we are the boys with no corn to hoe,
No cows to milk, and no grass to mow."
At night the farmer said: "Here's a trick
These roguish robins have had their pick."

## Cuckoo, Cuckoo, Cherry Tree (Traditional, Nursery Rhyme, PreS/K–5)

Cuckoo, cuckoo, cherry tree,
Catch a bird, and give it to me;
Let the tree be high or low,
Let it hail, or rain, or snow.

## Fairy Song (Thomas Randolph, Translated into English by Leigh Hunt, Poem, K–5/6+)

We the Fairies, blithe and antic,
Of dimensions not gigantic,
Though the moonshine mostly keep us,
Oft in orchards frisk and peep us.

Stolen sweets are always sweeter,
Stolen kisses much completer,
Stolen looks are nice in chapels,
Stolen, stolen be your apples.

When to bed the world is bobbing,
Then's the time for orchard-robbing;
Yet the fruit were scarce worth peeling
Were it not for stealing, stealing.

## Harvest Home (Traditional, Nursery Rhyme (Toast), K–5/6+)

Here's a health unto our master,
The founder of the feast,
And I hope to God with all my heart,
His soul in heaven may rest.
That everything may prosper
That ever he take in hand,
For we be all his servants,
And all at his command.

## Here Is a Tree (Traditional, Fingerplay, PreS/K–5)

Here is a tree with leaves so green. (Place arms together with hands spread apart.)
Here are the apples that hang between. (Hold out two fists.)
When the wind blows the apples will fall. (Wave arms back and forth and then bring them
    to ground.)
Here is a basket to gather them all. (Cup hands together.)

## How the Corn Grew (Emilie Poulsson, Fingerplay, K–5)

There was a field that waiting lay,
All hard and brown and bare;
There was a thrifty farmer came
And fenced it in with care, (Touch index fingers together.)

Then came a ploughman with his plough; (Place fingers on both hands together, leaving
    space between palms.)
From early until late,
Across the field and back again,
He ploughed the furrows straight. (Maintaining last position, move hands back and forth.)

The harrow* then was brought to make (Spread fingers and perform raking motion with
    both hands.)
The ground more soft and loose; And soon the farmer said with joy,
"My field is fit for use."

For many days the farmer then (Bend hand with fingers pointed downward for hoe.)
Was working with his hoe;
And little Johnny brought the corn
And dropped the kernels—so! (Pretend to drop kernels.)

And there they lay, until awaked
By tapping rains that fell, (Drum ground with fingers.)
Then pushed their green plumes up to greet (Hold hands straight, pointing upward.)
The sun they loved so well.

Then flocks and flocks of hungry crows
Came down the corn to taste;
But ba-ang! went the farmer's gun, (Hold left arm with right arm and snap right fingers.)
And off they flew in haste.

Then grew and grew the corn, until,
When autumn days had come,
With sickles keen they cut it down, (Curve right arm and pretend to cut corn.)
And sang the "Harvest Home."**

*Harrow: An agricultural tool that prepares the soil for planting. Harrowing often follows plowing.

*"Harvest Home": See entry before this one.

## I Had a Little Nut Tree (Traditional, Song, PreS/K–5)

I had a lit-tle nut tree, no-thing would it bear, But a sil-ver nut - meg and a gol - den pear; The king of Spain's daugh - ter came to vis - it me, And all was be cause of my lit - tle nut tree.

## Oats, Pease, Beans, and Barley (Traditional, Song, PreS/K–5)

Chorus:

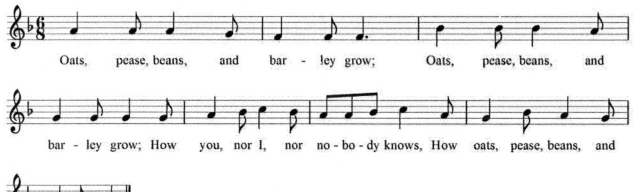

Oats, pease, beans, and bar - ley grow; Oats, pease, beans, and bar - ley grow; How you, nor I, nor no - bo - dy knows, How oats, pease, beans, and bar-ley grow.

Verse 1: First the farmer sows his seed,
Then he stands and takes his ease,
Stamps his foot, and claps his hands,
And turns about to view his lands.
(Repeat chorus.)

## Peter, Peter, Pumpkin Eater (Traditional, Nursery Rhyme, PreS/K–5)

Peter, Peter, pumpkin eater,
Had a wife and couldn't keep her;
He put her in a pumpkin shell
And there he kept her very well.

## Upon Paul's Steeple Stands a Tree (Traditional, Song, PreS/K–5)

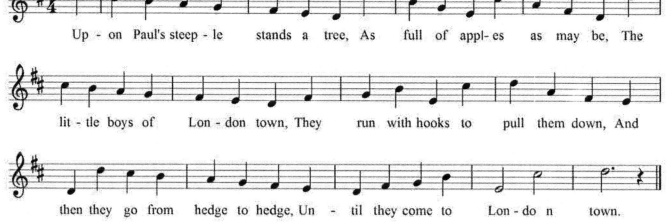

Up - on Paul's steep - le stands a tree, As full of appl- es as may be, The

lit - tle boys of Lon - don town, They run with hooks to pull them down, And

then they go from hedge to hedge, Un - til they come to Lon - do n town.

## Warm Hands Warm (Traditional, Song, PreS/K–5)

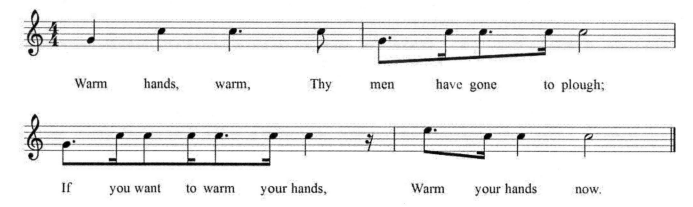

Warm hands, warm, Thy men have gone to plough;

If you want to warm your hands, Warm your hands now.

## Way Up High in an Apple Tree (Traditional, Fingerplay, PreS/K–5)

Way up high in an apple tree. (Point up.)
Two little apples smiled at me. (Show two fingers.)
I shook that tree as hard as I could, (Shake hands.)
Down came those apples— (Touch ground.)
Ummmm, they were good. (Rub tummy.)

# Autumn Holidays: Halloween

## And So They Went Along (Traditional, Nursery Rhyme, K–5/6+)

And so they went along,
To see what they could see.
And soon they saw a frog
A-sitting under a tree.
So—they—did.
One said it was a frog,
But the other said nay—
One said it was a canary-bird
With the feathers blown away.
So—it—was.

And so they went along,
To see what they could see,
And soon they saw a barn
A-standing by a tree.
One said it was a barn,
But the other said nay,
One said it was a meeting-house
With the steeple blown away.
And so they went along,
To see what they could see,
And soon they saw an owl,
A-sitting on a tree.
One said it was an owl,
But the other said nay,
One said it was the Evil One!
And they all ran away.

## The Fairy Thrall (Mary C. G. Byron, Poem, 6+)

On gossamer* nights when the moon is low,
And stars in the mist are hiding,
Over the hill where the foxgloves grow
You may see the fairies riding.
Kling! Klang! Kling!
Their stirrups and their bridles ring,
And their horns are loud and their bugles blow,
When the moon is low.

They sweep through the night like a whistling wind,
They pass and have left no traces;
But one of them lingers far behind
The flight of the fairy faces.
She makes no moan,
She sorrows in the dark alone,
She wails for the love of humankind,
Like a whistling wind.

"Ah! why did I roam where the elfins ride,
Their glimmering steps to follow?
They bore me far from my loved one's side,
To wander o'er hill and hollow.
Kling! Klang! Kling!
Their stirrups and their bridles ring,
But my heart is cold in the cold night-tide,
Where the elfins ride."

*Gossamer: Filmy, full of cobwebs.

## Five Little Goblins on a Halloween Night (Traditional, Fingerplay, PreS/K–5)

Five Little Goblins on a Halloween night
Made a very, very spooky sight.
The first one danced on his tippy-tip-toes. (Show first finger.)
The next one tumbled and bumped his nose. (Show second finger.)
The next one jumped high up in the air. (Show third finger.)
The next one sang a Halloween song. (Show fourth finger.)
The last little goblin played the whole night long. (Show thumb.)

## Five Little Pumpkins (Also known as "Five Little Jack-O-Lanterns," Traditional, Fingerplay, PreS/K–5)

Five little pumpkins sitting on a gate;
The first one said, "Oh my, it's getting late." (Show first finger.)
The second one said, "There are witches in the air." (Show second finger.)
The third one said, "But I don't care." (Show third finger.)
The fourth one said, "I'm ready for some fun!" (Show fourth finger.)
The fifth one said, "Let's run and run and run." (Show fifth finger.)
"Wooooooo" went the wind, And out went the lights. (Clap.)
And the five little pumpkins rolled out of sight. (Roll arms in a circular motion.)

## An Owl Sat Alone on the Branch of a Tree (Traditional, Nursery Rhyme, PreS/K–5)

An owl sat alone on the branch of a tree
And he was quiet as quiet could be.
'Twas night and his eyes were open like this
And he looked all around; not a thing did he miss
Some brownies climbed up the trunk of the tree
And sat on a branch as quiet as he.
Said the wise old owl, "To-Whoo, To-Whoo."
Up jumped the brownies and away they all flew.

# Autumn Holidays: Thanksgiving

## Five Fat Turkeys Are We (Traditional, Fingerplay, PreS/K–5)

Five fat turkeys are we. (Hold up right five fingers.)
We slept all night in a tree. (Hold right hand up high.)
When the cook came around, (Peer out under hand.)
We couldn't be found. (Shrug shoulders.)
So that's why we're here, you see. (Hold up right five fingers again.)

## Five little Pilgrims (Traditional, Fingerplay, PreS/K–5)

Five little Pilgrims on Thanksgiving Day:
The first one said, "I'll have cake if I may." (Show first finger.)
The second one said, "I'll have turkey roasted." (Show second finger.)
The third one said, "I'll have chestnuts toasted." (Show third finger.)
The fourth one said, "I'll have pumpkin pie." (Show fourth finger.)
The fifth one said, "Oh, cranberries I spy." (Show fifth finger.)
But before the Pilgrims ate their turkey dressing,
They bowed their heads and said a Thanksgiving blessing. (Place hands together as if in
    prayer.)

## I Met a Turkey Gobbler (Traditional, Nursery Rhyme, PreS/K–5)

I met a turkey gobbler
When I went out to play.
"Mr. Turkey Gobbler,
How are you today?"
"Gobble, gobble, gobble,

That I cannot say.
Don't ask me such a question
On Thanksgiving Day."

## Over the River and Through the Wood (Lydia Maria Child, Song, PreS/K–5)

Verse 3: Over the river and through the wood,
To have a first rate play;
Oh, hear the bell ring,
"Ting-a-ling-ling!" Hurrah for
Thanksgiving Day-ay!

From *Big Book of Seasons, Holidays, and Weather: Rhymes, Fingerplays, and Songs for Children*
by Elizabeth Cothen Low. Santa Barbara, CA: Libraries Unlimited. Copyright © 2011.

Verse 4: Over the river and through the wood,
Trot fast, my dapple* gray!
Spring over the ground,
Like a hunting hound!
For this is Thanksgiving Day.

Verse 5: Over the river and through the wood,
And straight through the barnyard gate.
We seem to go extremely slow
It is so hard to wait!

Verse 6: Over the river and through the wood,
Now Grandmother's face I spy.
Hurray for the fun, is the pudding done?
Hurrah for the pumpkin pie.

*Dapple: Spotted.

## Turkey Is a Funny Bird (Traditional, Fingerplay, PreS/K–5)

The turkey is a funny bird, (Spread out five fingers on hand with thumb extended.)
His head goes wobble, wobble, (Move thumb back and forth.)
And he knows just one word:
Gobble, gobble, gobble. (Bring thumb and fingers of right hand together in "talking" motion.)

# Autumn: Moon

## All Hail to the Moon (Traditional, Nursery Rhyme, K–5/6+)

All hail to the moon, all hail to thee!
I, pray thee, good moon, reveal to me
This night who my husband must be!

## Girls and Boys, Come Out to Play (Traditional, Nursery Rhyme, PreS/K–5)

Girls and boys, come out to play,
The moon doth shine as bright as day;
Leave your supper, and leave your sleep,
And come with your playfellows into the street.
Come with a whoop, come with a call,
Come with a good will or not at all.
Up the ladder and down the wall,

From *Big Book of Seasons, Holidays, and Weather: Rhymes, Fingerplays, and Songs for Children* by Elizabeth Cothen Low. Santa Barbara, CA: Libraries Unlimited. Copyright © 2011.

A halfpenny roll will serve us all.
You find milk, and I'll find flour,
And we'll have a pudding in half an hour.

## I See the Moon, and the Moon Sees Me (Traditional, Nursery Rhyme, PreS/K–5)

I see the moon, and the moon sees me,
God bless the moon, and God bless me.

## The Man in the Moon (Traditional, Nursery Rhyme, PreS/K–5)

The man in the moon,
Came down too soon,
And ask'd his way to Norwich;
He went by the south
And burnt his mouth
With eating cold pease-porridge.

## The Man in the Moon Drinks Claret (Traditional, Nursery Rhyme, K–5/6+)

The Man in the Moon drinks claret,*
With powder-beef, turnip, and carrot.

*Claret: A kind of red wine.

## The Man in the Moon Looked Out of the Moon (Traditional, Nursery Rhyme, PreS/K–5)

The man in the moon looked out of the moon
Looked out of the moon and said . . .
'Tis time for all good children on Earth
To think about going to bed!

## The Man on the Moon (Traditional, Nursery Rhyme, PreS/K–5)

The Man on the Moon as he sails the sky
Is a very remarkable skipper,
But he made a mistake when he tried to take
A drink of milk from the Dipper.

He dipped right out of the Milky Way,
And slowly and carefully filled it,
The Big Bear growled, and the Little Bear howled
And frightened him so that he spilled it!

## The Moon (Eliza Lee Fallen, Poem, K–5)

O, look at the moon!
She is shining up there;
O mother, she looks
Like a lamp in the air.

Last week she was smaller,
And shaped like a bow;
But now she's grown bigger,
And round as an O.

Pretty moon, pretty moon,
How you shine on the door,
And make it all bright
On my nursery floor!

You shine on my playthings,
And show me their place,
And I love to look up
At your pretty bright face.

And there is a star
Close by you, and maybe
That small twinkling star
Is your little baby.

## Moon, So Round and Yellow (Matthias Barr, Poem, K–5)

Moon, so round and yellow,
Looking from on high,
How I love to see you
Shining in the sky.
Oft and oft I wonder,
When I see you there,
How they get to light you,
Hanging in the air:

Where you go at morning,
When the night is past,
And the sun comes peeping
O'er the hills at last.
Sometime I will watch you
Slyly overhead,
When you think I'm sleeping
Snugly in my bed.

## New Moon, New Moon (Traditional, Nursery Rhyme, K–5/6+)

New moon, new moon, declare to me:
Shall I this night my true love see?
Not in his best, but in the array
As he walks in every day.

## New Moon, New Moon, I Hail Thee! (Traditional, Nursery Rhyme, K–5/6+)

New moon, new moon, I hail thee!
By all the virtue in thy body,
Grant this night that I may see
He who my true love is to be.

## One Moonshiny Night (Traditional, Nursery Rhyme, K–5/6+)

One moonshiny night
As I sat high,
Waiting for one
To come by;

The boughs did bend,
My heart did ache
To see what hole the fox did make.

## There Were Three Jovial Welshmen (Traditional, Nursery Rhyme, K–5/6+)

There were three jovial Welshmen,
As I have heard them say,
And they would go a-hunting
Upon St. David's Day.
All the day they hunted,
And nothing could they find
But a ship a-sailing,

A-sailing with the wind.
One said it was a ship,
The other he said, nay;
The third said it was a house,
With the chimney blown away.
And all the night they hunted,
And nothing could they find
But the moon a-gliding,
A-gliding with the wind.
One said it was the moon,
The other he said, nay;
The third said it was a cheese,
And half of it cut away.

## The Satyrs and the Moon (Herbert S. Gorman, Poem, 6+)

Within the wood behind the hill
The moon got tangled in the trees.
Her splendor made the branches thrill
And thrilled the breeze.

The satyrs in the grotto bent
Their heads to see the wondrous sight.
"It is a god in banishment
That stirs the night."

The little satyr looked and guessed:
"It is an apple that one sees,
Brought from that garden of the West—
Hesperides."*

"It is a cyclops' glaring eye."
"A temple dome from Babylon."
"A Titan's cup of ivory."
"A little sun."

The tiny satyr jumped for joy,
And kicked hoofs in utmost glee.
"It is a wondrous silver toy—
Bring it to me!"

A great wind whistled through the blue
And caught the moon and tossed it high;
A bubble of pale fire it flew
Across the sky.

From *Big Book of Seasons, Holidays, and Weather: Rhymes, Fingerplays, and Songs for Children* by Elizabeth Cothen Low. Santa Barbara, CA: Libraries Unlimited. Copyright © 2011.

The satyrs gasped and looked and smiled,
And wagged their heads from side to side,
Except their shaggy little child,
Who cried and cried.

\* Hesperides: A mythological garden tended by nymphs.

## There Was an Old Woman (Traditional, Nursery Rhyme, PreS/K–5)

There was an old woman tossed up in a basket,
Nineteen times as high as the moon;
Where she was going I couldn't but ask it,
For in her hand she carried a broom.
"Old woman, old woman, old woman," quoth I,
"O whither, O whither, O whither so high?"
"To brush the cobwebs off the sky!"
"Shall I go with thee?" "Ay, by and by."

# Autumn Weather: Clouds/Fog

## A Hill Full (Traditional, Riddle, K–5/6+)

A hill full, a hole full,
Ye cannot catch a bowl full.

Answer: The mist.

## Banks Full (Traditional, Riddle, K–5/6+)

Banks full, braes\* full,
Though ye gather all day,
Ye'll not gather your hands full.

Answer: The mist.
\*Braes: A hillside.

## A Northern Har (Traditional, Saying, K–5/6+)

A northern har\*
Brings drought from far.

\*Har: A mist or thick fog.

## One Misty Misty Morning (Traditional, Nursery Rhyme, K–5/6+)

One misty, misty morning,
When cloudy was the weather,
I met a little old man
Clothed all in leather;
He began to bow and scrape,
And I began to grin,
How do you do, and how do you do,
And how do you do again?

*See also* "Sing, Little Bird" (Traditional, PreS/K–5) in "The Four Seasons" chapter, weather section.

## When Clouds Appear (Traditional, Saying, K–5/6+)

When clouds appear like rocks and towers,
The earth's refreshed by frequent showers.

## White Sheep (Traditional, Riddle, K–5/6+)

White sheep, white sheep,
On a blue hill,
When the wind stops,
You all stand still.
When the wind blows,
You walk away slow.
White sheep, white sheep,
Where do you go?

Answer: Clouds.

# Winter

The entries in this section are about winter and related subjects, such as snowy weather. Holidays occurring during winter are also included.

## Bread and Milk (Christina Rossetti, Poem, PreS/K–5)

Bread and milk for breakfast,
And woolen frocks to wear,
And a crumb for robin redbreast
On the cold days of the year.

## Cold and Raw the North Wind Doth Blow (Traditional, Nursery Rhyme, K–5/6+)

Cold and raw the north wind doth blow,
Bleak in the morning early;
All the hills are covered with snow,
And winter's now come fairly.

## The Cottager to Her Infant (Dorothy Wordsworth, Poem, K–5/6+)

The days are cold, the nights are long,
The north-wind sings a doleful song;
Then hush again upon my breast;
All merry things are now at rest,
Save thee, my pretty love!


The kitten sleeps upon the hearth;
The crickets long have ceased their mirth;
There's nothing stirring in the house
Save one wee, hungry, nibbling mouse;
Then why so busy, thou?


Nay! start not at that sparkling light;
'Tis but the moon that shines so bright
On the window-pane bedropped with rain.
There, little darling! sleep again,
And wake when it is day!

*See also* "The Fairy Book" (Norman Gale, K–5/6+) in "The Four Seasons" chapter.
*See also* "The Garden Year" (Sara Coleridge, K–5/6+) in "The Four Seasons" chapter.

## Goodby and Keep Cold (Robert Frost, Poem, 6+)

This saying good-by on the edge of the dark
And cold to an orchard so young in the bark
Reminds me of all that can happen to harm
An orchard away at the end of the farm
All winter, cut off by a hill from the house.
I don't want it girdled by rabbit and mouse,
I don't want it dreamily nibbled for browse
By deer, and I don't want it budded by grouse.
(If certain it wouldn't be idle to call
I'd summon grouse, rabbit, and deer to the wall
And warn them away with a stick for a gun.)
I don't want it stirred by the heat of the sun.
(We made it secure against being, I hope,
By setting it out on a northerly slope.)
No orchard's the worse for the wintriest storm;
But one thing about it, it mustn't get warm.
"How often already you've had to be told,
Keep cold, young orchard. Good-by and keep cold.

Dread fifty above more than fifty below."
I have to be gone for a season or so.
My business awhile is with different trees,
Less carefully nourished, less fruitful than these,
And such as is done to their wood with an ax—
Maples and birches and tamaracks.
I wish I could promise to lie in the night
And think of an orchard's arboreal plight
When slowly (and nobody comes with a light)
Its heart sinks lower under the sod.
But something has to be left to God.

## Here We Go Round the Mulberry Bush (Traditional, Song, PreS/K–5)

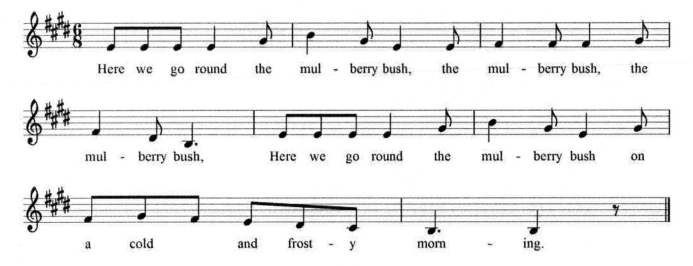

Verse 2: This is the way we wash our clothes,
Wash our clothes, wash our clothes:
This is the way we wash our clothes
On a cold, frosty morning!

Verse 3: This is the way we clean our rooms,
Clean our rooms, clean our rooms:
This is the way we clean our rooms
On a cold, frosty morning!

*See also* "The Human Seasons" (John Keats, 6+) in "The Four Seasons" chapter.

## I'm Called by the Name of a Man (Traditional, Riddle, K–5/6+)

I'm called by the name of a man.
Yet am as little as a mouse;
When winter comes I love to be
With my red target near the house.

Answer: Robin.

## Jack Frost (Gabriel Setoun, Poem, 6+)

The door was shut, as doors should be,
Before you went to bed last night;
Yet Jack Frost has got in, you see,
And left your window silver white.

He must have waited till you slept;
And not a single word he spoke,
But penciled o'er the panes and crept
Away again before you woke.

And now you cannot see the hills
Nor fields that stretch beyond the lane;
But there are fairer things than these
His fingers traced on every pane.

Rocks and castles towering high;
Hills and dales, and streams and fields;
And knights in armor riding by,
With nodding plumes and shining shields.

And here are little boats, and there
Big ships with sails spread to the breeze;
And yonder, palm trees waving fair
On islands set in silver seas.

And butterflies with gauzy wings;
And herds of cows and flocks of sheep;
And fruit and flowers and all the things
You see when you are sound asleep.

For creeping softly underneath
The door when all the lights are out,
Jack Frost takes every breath you breathe,
And knows the things you think about.

He paints them on the window pane
In fairy lines with frozen steam;
And when you wake you see again
The lovely things you saw in dream.

*See also* "January Cold Desolate" (Christina Rossetti, K–5/6+) in "The Four Seasons" chapter.
*See also* "Lazy Lawrence" (Traditional, PreS/K–5) in "The Four Seasons" chapter.

## Let's Put on Our Mittens (Traditional, Fingerplay, PreS/K–5)

Let's put on our mittens (Pretend to put on mittens.)
And button our coats; (Pretend to button coats.)
Wrap a scarf snuggly (Pretend to wrap scarf around neck.)
Around our throats.
Pull on our boots, (Pretend to put on boots.)
Fasten the straps.
And tie on tightly,
Our warm winter caps. (Pretend to put on hat.)
Then open the door, (Mime opening door.)
And out we go
Into the soft and feathery snow.

## Little Cock Robin (Traditional, Nursery Rhyme, PreS/K–5)

Little cock robin peeped out of his cabin,
To see the cold winter come in,
Tit, for tat, what matter for that,
He'll hide his head under his wing!

## Little John Jiggy Jag (Traditional, Nursery Rhyme, K–5/6+)

Little John Jiggy Jag,
He rode a penny nag,
And went to Wigan to woo.
When he came to a beck,
He fell and broke his neck,
—Johnny, how dost thou now?
I made him a hat,

Of my coat-lap,
And stockings of pearly blue:
A hat and a feather,
To keep out cold weather;
—So, Johnny, how dost thou now?

## Oh! Where Do Fairies Hide Their Heads? (Thomas Haynes Bayly, Poem, K–5/6+)

Oh! where do fairies hide their heads,
When snow lies on the hills,
When frost has spoiled their mossy beds,
And crystallized their rills?*
Beneath the moon they cannot trip
In circles o'er the plain;
And draughts of dew they cannot sip,
Till green leaves come again.
Perhaps, in small, blue diving-bells
They plunge beneath the waves,
Inhabiting the wreathed shells
That lie in coral caves.
Perhaps, in red Vesuvius**
Carousals they maintain;
And cheer their little spirits thus,
Till green leaves come again.


When they return, there will be mirth
And music in the air.
And fairy wings upon the earth,
And mischief everywhere.
The maids, to keep the elves aloof,
Will bar the doors in vain;
No key-hole will be fairy-proof
When green leaves come again.


*Rills: Tiny streams.
**Vesuvius: A volcano in Italy.

## The Polar Bear (Hilaire Belloc, Poem, K–5/6+)

The Polar Bear is unaware
Of cold that cuts me through:
For why? He has a coat of hair,
I wish I had one too!

*See also* "The Seasons" (Traditional, K–5/6+) in "The Four Seasons" chapter.
*See also* "Sing, Little Bird" (Traditional, PreS/K–5) in "The Four Seasons" chapter, weather section.

## Shoe, Shoe My Little Horse (Traditional, Nursery Rhyme, K–5/6+)

Shoe, shoe my little horse,
To-morrow it will be frosty;
Then will horse-shoes be dear,
Two will cost a stiver.*

*Stiver: Dutch currency, about 5 cents.

*See also* "Thirty Days Hath September" (Traditional, K–5/6+) in "The Four Seasons" chapter.

## This Is the Squirrel (Traditional, Action Rhyme, PreS/K–5)

This is the squirrel
With eyes so bright, (Point to eyes.)
Hunting for nuts
With all his might. (Pretend to dig in ground.)
This is the hole (Touch thumb and index finger of right hand together, leaving a hole in the
        middle.)
Where day by day,
Nut after nut.
He stores away. (Use left hand to pretend to place nuts in "hole.")
When winter comes
With its cold and storm,
He'll sleep curled up, (Hug arms and curl up body.)
All snug and warm.

## Warm Hands, Warm (Traditional, Nursery Rhyme, PreS/K–5)

Warm hands, warm,
Thy men are gone to plough;
If you want to warm your hands,
Warm your hands now.

## Winter Night (Mary F. Butts, Poem, K–5/6+)

Blow, wind, blow!
Drift the flying snow!
Send it twirling, whirling overhead!
There's a bedroom in a tree
Where, snug as snug can be,
The squirrel nests in his cozy bed.

Shriek, wind, shriek!
Make the branches creak!
Battle with the boughs till break o' day!
In a snow-cave warm and tight,
Through the icy winter night
The rabbit sleeps the peaceful hours away.

Call, wind, call!
In entry and in hall!
Straight from off the mountain white and wild!
Soft purrs the pussy-cat,
On her little fluffy mat,
And beside her nestles close her furry child.

Scold, wind, scold!
So bitter and so bold!
Shake the windows with your tap, tap, tap!
With half-shut dreamy eyes
The drowsy baby lies
Cuddled closely in his mother's lap.

## Winter's Thunder (Traditional, Nursery Rhyme, K–5/6+)

Winter's thunder
Is the world's wonder.
From Lancashire.*

*Lancashire: Area in northwest England.

### Away in a Manger (Traditional, Song, PreS/K–5/6+)

A way in a man-ger, no crib for His bed, The lit-tle Lord Je-sus
lay down His sweet head. The stars in the heav-ens
looked down where He lay. The lit-tle Lord Je-sus, a-sleep in the hay.

Verse 2: The cattle are lowing, the poor Baby wakes.
But little Lord Jesus, no crying He makes.
I love thee, Lord Jesus, look down from the sky,
And stay by the cradle till morning is nigh.

### Bounce Buckram (Traditional, Nursery Rhyme, PreS/K–5)

Bounce Buckram, velvet's dear;
Christmas comes but once a year.

### Christmas Comes But Once a Year (Traditional, Nursery Rhyme, K–5/6+)

Christmas comes but once a year,
And when it comes it brings good cheer:
A pocket full of money,
And a cellar full of beer,
And a good fat pig to last you all the year.

From *Big Book of Seasons, Holidays, and Weather: Rhymes, Fingerplays, and Songs for Children* by Elizabeth Cothen Low. Santa Barbara, CA: Libraries Unlimited. Copyright © 2011.

## Christmas Is Coming, the Geese Are Getting Fat (Traditional, Song, PreS/K–5)

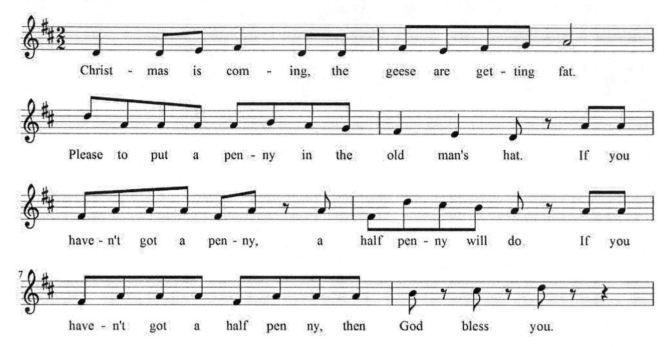

## Dame, Get Up and Bake Your Pies (Traditional, Song, K–5/6+)

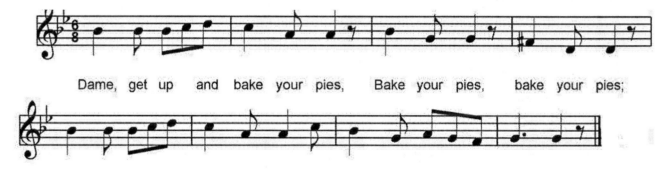

Verse 2: Dame, what makes your maidens lie,
Maidens lie, maidens lie;
Dame, what makes your maidens lie,
On Christmas day in the morning?

Verse 3: Dame, what makes your ducks to die,
Ducks to die, duck to die;
Dame, what makes your ducks to die,
On Christmas day in the morning?

Verse 4: Their wings are cut and they cannot fly,
Cannot fly, cannot fly;
Their wings are cut and they cannot fly,
On Christmas day in the morning.

## Deck the Halls (Traditional, Song, PreS/K–5/6+)

*From Big Book of Seasons, Holidays, and Weather: Rhymes, Fingerplays, and Songs for Children*
by Elizabeth Cothen Low. Santa Barbara, CA: Libraries Unlimited. Copyright © 2011.

## The Feast of the Snow (Gilbert Keith Chesterton, Poem, 6+)

There is heard a hymn when the panes are dim,
And never before or again,
When the nights are strong with a darkness long,
And the dark is alive with rain.
Never we know but in sleet and snow
The place where the great fires are,
That the midst of earth is a raging mirth,
And the heart of the earth a star.

And at night we win to the ancient inn,
Where the Child in the frost is furled,
We follow the feet where all souls meet,
At the inn at the end of the world.

The gods lie dead where the leaves lie red,
For the flame of the sun is flown;
The gods lie cold where the leaves are gold,
And a Child comes forth alone.

## The First Noel (Traditional, Song, PreS/K–5/6+)

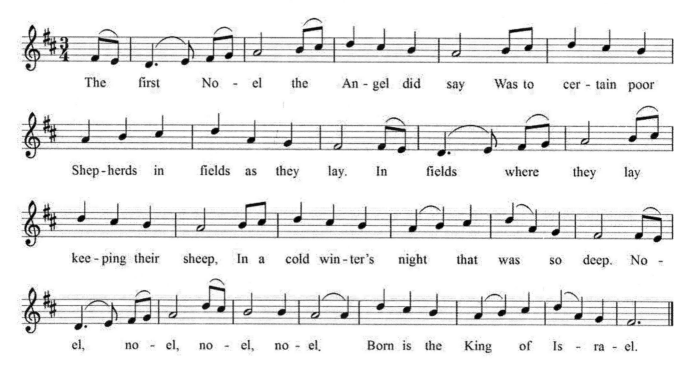

102

*From Big Book of Seasons, Holidays, and Weather: Rhymes, Fingerplays, and Songs for Children*
by Elizabeth Cothen Low. Santa Barbara, CA: Libraries Unlimited. Copyright © 2011.

## Five Little Bells (Traditional, Fingerplay, PreS/K–5)

Five little bells, hanging in a row, (Show five fingers.)
The first one said, "Ring me slow." (Show first finger.)
The second one said, "Ring me fast." (Show second finger.)
The third one said, "Ring me last." (Show third finger.)
The fourth one said, "I'm like a chime." (Show fourth finger.)
The fifth one said, "Ring me at Christmas Time." (Show fifth finger.)

## Five Little Reindeer (Traditional, Fingerplay, PreS/K–5)

One, two, three, four, five little reindeer, (Count out five fingers.)
Stood by the North Pole gate.
"Hurry, Santa," called the reindeer,
"Or we will all be late." (Point to wrist.)
One, two, three, four, five little reindeer, (Count out five fingers.)
Santa said, "Please wait!" (Hold out hand.)
"Wait for three more little reindeers, (Count out three fingers on other hand.)"
    Then we will have eight." (Show eight fingers.)

## Go Tell It on the Mountain (Traditional, Song, PreS/K–5/6+)

Go tell it on the moun - tain o ver the hills and eve-ry-wh-ere.

Go tell it on the moun - tain that Je sus Christ is born! While

shep herds kept their watch o'er si lent flocks by night. Be -

hold through out the heav -en there shone a Ho ly light.

From *Big Book of Seasons, Holidays, and Weather: Rhymes, Fingerplays, and Songs for Children* by Elizabeth Cothen Low. Santa Barbara, CA: Libraries Unlimited. Copyright © 2011.

## God Bless the Master of This House (Traditional, Nursery Rhyme (Toast), K–5/6+)

God bless the master of this house,
The mistress also,
And all the little children
That round the table go;
And all your kin and kinsmen,
That dwell both far and near;
I wish you a merry Christmas,
And a happy new year.

## Here Is the Chimney (Traditional, Fingerplay, PreS/K–5)

Here is a chimney. (Hold out right fist with thumb tucked in on top.)
Here is a top. (Place left hand, palm down, on right fist,)
Open the cover, (Remove left hand.)
Out Santa Claus pops. (Pop out right thumb.)

## Jingle Bells (Traditional, Song, B/PreS/K–5)

Verse 1: Dashing through the snow
In a one-horse open sleigh
O'er the fields we go
Laughing all the way
Bells on bobtail ring
Making spirits bright
What fun it is to ride and sing
A sleighing song tonight!
Chorus:

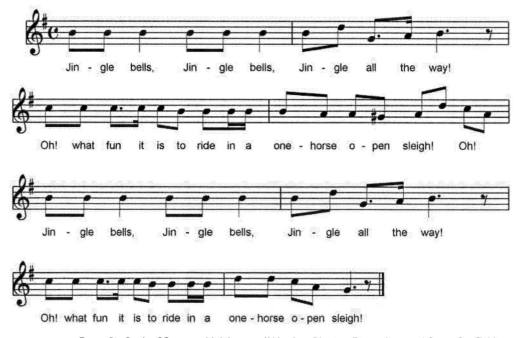

Verse 2: A day or two ago
I thought I'd take a ride;
And soon Miss Fannie Bright
Was seated by my side.
The horse was lean and lank;
Misfortune seemed his lot;
He got into a drifted bank,
And we, we got upsot.*

(Repeat chorus.)

Verse 3: Now the ground is white,
Go it while you're young;
Take the girls tonight,
And sing this sleighing song.
Just get a bobtailed bay,**
Two-forty for his speed;
Then hitch him to an open sleigh,
And crack! You'll take the lead.

(Repeat chorus.)

*Upsot: Overturned.
**Bay: A reddish-brown horse.

## Joy to the World (Traditional, Song, PreS/K–5/6+)

## I Saw Three Ships (Traditional, Song, PreS/K–5/6+)

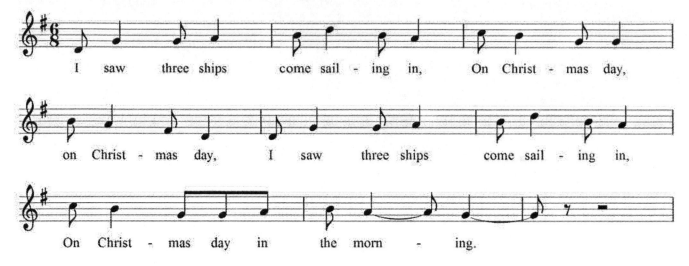

I saw three ships come sail - ing in, On Christ - mas day, on Christ - mas day, I saw three ships come sail - ing in, On Christ - mas day in the morn - ing.

Verse 2: And what was in those ships all three?
On Christmas day, on Christmas day,
And what was in those ships all three?
On Christmas day in the morning.

Verse 3: Our Savior Christ and his lady
On Christmas day, on Christmas day,
Our Savior Christ and his lady,
On Christmas day in the morning.

Verse 4: Pray whither sailed those ships all three?
On Christmas day, on Christmas day,
Pray whither sailed those ships all three?
On Christmas day in the morning.

Verse 5: Oh, they sailed into Bethlehem,
On Christmas day, on Christmas day,
Oh, they sailed into Bethlehem,
On Christmas day in the morning.

Verse 6: And all the bells on earth shall ring,
On Christmas day, on Christmas day,
And all the bells on earth shall ring,
On Christmas day in the morning.

From *Big Book of Seasons, Holidays, and Weather: Rhymes, Fingerplays, and Songs for Children* by Elizabeth Cothen Low. Santa Barbara, CA: Libraries Unlimited. Copyright © 2011.

Verse 7: And all the Angels in Heaven shall sing,
On Christmas day, on Christmas day,
And all the Angels in Heaven shall sing,
On Christmas day in the morning.

Verse 8: And all the souls on earth shall sing,
On Christmas day, on Christmas day,
And all the souls on earth shall sing,
On Christmas day in the morning.

Verse 9: Then let us all rejoice, amen,
On Christmas day, on Christmas day,
Then let us all rejoice, amen,
On Christmas day in the morning.

## Jack Horner Was a Pretty Lad (Traditional, Nursery Rhyme, K–5/6+)

Jack Horner was a pretty lad,
Near London he did dwell,
His father's heart he made full glad,
His mother loved him well.
While little Jack was sweet and young,
If he by chance should cry,
His mother pretty sonnets sung,
With a lul-la-ba-by,
With such a dainty curious tone,
As Jack sat on her knee,
So that, e'er he could go alone,
He sung as well as she.
A pretty boy of curious wit,
All people spoke his praise,
And in the corner would he sit
In Christmas holy days.
When friends they did together meet,
To pass away the time—
Why, little Jack, he sure would eat
His Christmas pie in rhyme.
And said, Jack Horner, in the corner,
Eats good Christmas pie,
And with his thumbs pulls out the plumbs,
And said, "Good boy am I!"

## Little Jack Horner (Traditional, Nursery Rhyme, PreS/K–5)

Little Jack Horner
Sat in the corner,
Eating a Christmas pie.
He put in his thumb,
And he took out a plum,
And said, " What a good boy am I!"

## O Christmas Tree (Traditional, Song, PreS/K–5)

O Christ-mas tree, O Christ-mas tree, How love-ly are your branch-es! O

Christ-mas tree, O Christ - ms tree, How love-ly are your brach-es! In

Beau-ty green will al - ways grow, Through sum-mer sun and win-ter snow. O

Christ-mas tree, O Christ-mas tree, How love-ly are your branch-es!

## O Little Town of Bethlehem (Phillips Brooks, Song, PreS/K–5)

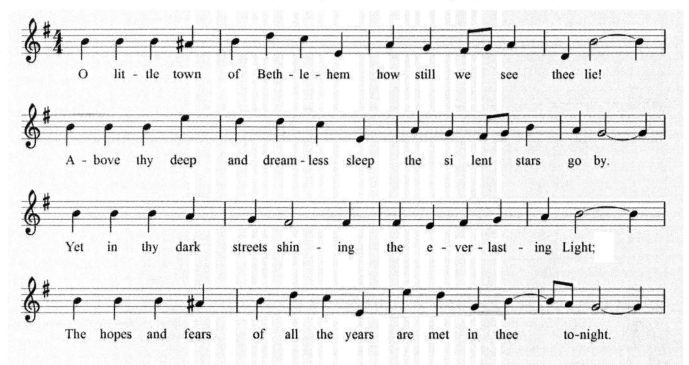

O lit - tle town of Beth - le - hem how still we see thee lie!

A - bove thy deep and dream - less sleep the si lent stars go by.

Yet in thy dark streets shin - ing the e - ver - last - ing Light;

The hopes and fears of all the years are met in thee to-night.

Verse 2: For Christ is born of Mary,
And, gathered all above,
While mortals sleep, the angels keep
Their watch of wondering love.
O morning stars, together
Proclaim the holy birth!
And praises sing to God the King,
And peace to men on earth.

Verse 3: How silently, how silently,
The wondrous gift is given!
So God imparts to human hearts
The blessings of His heaven.
No ear may hear His coming,
But in this world of sin,
Where meek souls will receive Him still,
The dear Christ enters in.

Verse 4: O holy Child of Bethlehem!
Descend to us, we pray;
Cast out our sin, and enter in,
Be born in us to-day.

From *Big Book of Seasons, Holidays, and Weather: Rhymes, Fingerplays, and Songs for Children*
by Elizabeth Cothen Low. Santa Barbara, CA: Libraries Unlimited. Copyright © 2011.

We hear the Christmas angels
The great glad tidings tell;
Oh come to us, abide with us,
Our Lord Emmanuel!

## On Christmas Eve (Traditional, Nursery Rhyme, PreS/K–5)

On Christmas Eve I turned the spit,
I burnt my fingers, I feel it yet;
The cock sparrow flew over the table;
The pot began to play with the ladle.

## Santa Claus (Emilie Poulsson, Fingerplay, PreS/K–5)

O, clap, clap the hands, (Clap hands.)
And sing out with glee!
For Christmas is coming, and merry are we!
Now swift o'er the snow
The tiny reindeer (Link thumbs and tap fingers on ground.)
Are trotting and bringing
Good Santa Claus near. (Point thumb up and make fist with right hand.)

O, clap, clap the hands, (Clap hands.)
And sing out with glee!
For Christmas is coming, and merry are we!
Our stockings we'll hang, (Point hand downward to depict "stocking.")
And while we're asleep
Then down thro' the chimney (Put one fist on top of other.)
Will Santa Claus creep.

O, clap, clap the hands, (Clap hands.)
And sing out with glee!
For Christmas is coming, and merry are we!
He'll empty his pack,
Then up he will come. (Point thumb up and make fist with right hand. Place left fist under-
    neath right one.)
And calling the reindeer,
Will haste away home.

## See All the Presents (Traditional, Fingerplay, PreS/K–5)

See all the presents by the Christmas tree.
Some for you (Point to audience.)

And some for me. (Point to own chest.)
Long ones, (Stretch out arms wide.)
Tall ones, (Stretch arm up high.)
Short ones, too. (Place hands only a few inches apart.)
And here is a round one (Form circle with arms.)
Wrapped in blue.
Isn't it fun to look and see
All the presents by the Christmas tree?

## Silent Night (Traditional, Song, PreS/K–5/6+)

Si - lent night! Ho - ly night! All is calm, all is bright,

Round yon Vir - gin Moth - er and Child! Ho - ly In - fant, so

ten - der and mild, Sleep in heav - en - ly pea - ce, Sleep in heav - en - ly

peace.

## 'Twas the Night Before Christmas (Clement Clarke Moore, Poem, PreS/K–5/6+)

'Twas the night before Christmas, when all through the house
Not a creature was stirring, not even a mouse.
The stockings were hung by the chimney with care,
In hopes that St. Nicholas soon would be there.
The children were nestled all snug in their beds,
While visions of sugar-plums danced in their heads.
And mamma in her 'kerchief, and I in my cap,
Had just settled our brains for a long winter's nap,
When out on the lawn there arose such a clatter,
I sprang from the bed to see what was the matter.

Away to the window I flew like a flash,
Tore open the shutters and threw up the sash.
The moon on the breast of the new-fallen snow
Gave the luster of midday to objects below;
When, what to my wondering eyes should appear,
But a miniature sleigh, and eight tiny reindeer,
With a little old driver, so lively and quick,
I knew in a moment it must be St. Nick.
More rapid than eagles his coursers they came,
And he whistled, and shouted, and called them by name;
"Now, Dasher! Now, Dancer! Now, Prancer and Vixen!
On, Comet! On Cupid! On, Donder and Blitzen!
To the top of the porch! To the top of the wall!
Now dash away! Dash away! Dash away all!"
As dry leaves that before the wild hurricane fly,
When they meet with an obstacle, mount to the sky,
So up to the house-top the coursers they flew,
With the sleigh full of toys, and St. Nicholas too.
And then, in a twinkling, I heard on the roof
The prancing and pawing of each little hoof.
As I drew in my head, and was turning around,
Down the chimney St. Nicholas came with a bound.
He was dressed all in fur, from his head to his foot,
And his clothes were all tarnished with ashes and soot;
A bundle of toys he had flung on his back,
And he looked like a peddler just opening his pack.
His eyes—how they twinkled! His dimples how merry!
His cheeks were like roses, his nose like a cherry!
His droll little mouth was drawn up like a bow,
And the beard of his chin was as white as the snow;
The stump of a pipe he held tight in his teeth,
And the smoke it encircled his head like a wreath.
He had a broad face and a little round belly,
That shook, when he laughed, like a bowlful of jelly.
He was chubby and plump, a right jolly old elf,
And I laughed when I saw him, in spite of myself;
A wink of his eye and a twist of his head,
Soon gave me to know I had nothing to dread;
He spoke not a word, but went straight to his work,
And filled all the stockings; then turned with a jerk,
And laying his finger aside of his nose,
And giving a nod, up the chimney he rose;
He sprang to his sleigh, to his team gave a whistle,

And away they all flew like the down of a thistle.
But I heard him exclaim, ere he drove out of sight,
"Happy Christmas to all, and to all a goodnight."

## The Twelve Days of Christmas (Traditional, Song, PreS/K–5/6+)

On    the    first    day    of    Christ - mas,    my    true    love    gave    to    me,    a

par - tridge    in a pear tree.

Verse 2: The second day of Christmas,
My true love sent to me,
Two turtledoves, and
A partridge in a pear tree.

Verse 3: The third day of Christmas,
My true love sent to me,
Three French hens . . . (Continue with other gifts: two turtle doves and a partridge in a
        pear tree.)

Verse 4: The fourth day of Christmas,
My true love sent to me,
Four calling birds . . . (Continue with other gifts.)

Verse 5: The fifth day of Christmas,
My true love sent to me,
Five gold rings . . . (Continue with other gifts.)

Verse 6: The sixth day of Christmas,
My true love sent to me,
Six geese a-laying . . . (Continue with other gifts.)

Verse 7: The seventh day of Christmas,
My true love sent to me,
Seven swans a-swimming . . . (Continue with other gifts.)

*From Big Book of Seasons, Holidays, and Weather: Rhymes, Fingerplays, and Songs for Children*
by Elizabeth Cothen Low. Santa Barbara, CA: Libraries Unlimited. Copyright © 2011.

Verse 8: The eighth day of Christmas,
My true love sent to me,
Eight maids a-milking . . . (Continue with other gifts.)

Verse 9: The ninth day of Christmas,
My true love sent to me,
Nine drummers drumming . . . (Continue with other gifts.)

Verse 10: The tenth day of Christmas,
My true love sent to me,
Ten pipers piping . . . (Continue with other gifts.)

Verse 11: The eleventh day of Christmas,
My true love sent to me,
Eleven ladies dancing . . . (Continue with other gifts.)

Verse 12: The twelfth day of Christmas,
My true love sent to me,
Twelve lords a-leaping . . . (Continue with other gifts.)

# Winter Holidays: Hanukkah

## Dreidel Song (Samuel S. Grossman, Song, PreS/K–5/6+)

From *Big Book of Seasons, Holidays, and Weather: Rhymes, Fingerplays, and Songs for Children* by Elizabeth Cothen Low. Santa Barbara, CA: Libraries Unlimited. Copyright © 2011.

Verse 2: It has a lovely body,
With legs so short and thin,
And when it gets all tired,
It drops and then I win.

(Repeat chorus.)

Verse 3 My dreidel is so playful,
It loves to dance and spin,
A happy game of dreidel,
Come play now, let's begin.

(Repeat chorus.)

Verse 4: It has a lovely body,
With legs so short and thin,
And when it gets all tired,
It drops and then I win.

## Winter Holidays: New Year's Day

### Auld Lang Syne* (Robert Burns, Song, K–5/6+)

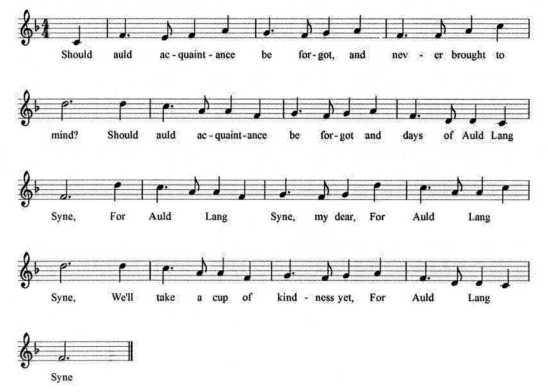

*Auld lang syne: Good old times.

From *Big Book of Seasons, Holidays, and Weather: Rhymes, Fingerplays, and Songs for Children*
by Elizabeth Cothen Low. Santa Barbara, CA: Libraries Unlimited. Copyright © 2011.

## Richard of Dalton Dale (Traditional, Nursery Rhyme, 6+)

On New-Year's-day, as I've heard say,
Richard he mounted his dapple grey;
He put on his roast-beef clothes,
His shoes, his buckles, and his hose,
Likewise his hat upon his head,
Stuck all round with ribbons red!
Thus rode Richard of Dalton Dale
To the parson's house to court Mrs. Jane.
Richard he rode across the moor,
Until he came to the parson's door,
Where he did knock both loud and fast,
Till he made the company amazed at last.
A trusty servant let him in,
His pleasant courtship to begin.
Richard he strutted about the hall,
And aloud for Mrs. Jane did call.
Mrs. Jane came down straightway
To hear what Richard had got to say;
He scraped his leg and kissed his hand,
"I am," said he—don't you understand?
"Mrs. Jane, I fain would know
Whether you'll be my bride or no!"
"Richard, if I'm to be your bride,
Pray what for a living will you provide?
For I can neither card nor spin,
Nor ever in my life, could do any such thing."
"Sometimes I reap, sometimes I mow,
And sometimes I to the market go;
With Goodman's hogs, or corn, or hay,
I addle my ninepence every day."
"Ninepence a day will never do,
For I wear silks and satins too;
Ninepence a day won't keep us with meat,
Odd zooks! could you think of a crown a week?"
"There is an old house that stands hard by,
It'll be all my own when my grandfather die,
And if you'll consent to marry me now,
I'll feed you as fat as my grandfather's sow."
Richard's compliments did so delight,
That the company set up a laugh outright;
So Richard having no more to say,
Mounted his keffin* and rode away.

*Keffin: A horse.

### Little Maid, Little Maid (Traditional, Nursery Rhyme, PreS/K–5)

Little maid, little maid, turn the pin,
Open the door and let us come in;
God be here, God be there.
I wish you all a happy new year!

## Winter Holidays: Valentine's Day

### Five Little Valentines (Traditional, Fingerplay, PreS/K–5)

Five little valentines were having a race.
The first little valentine was frilly with lace. (Hold up thumb.)
The second little valentine had a funny face. (Hold up second finger.)
The third little valentine said, "I love you." (Hold up third finger.)
The fourth little valentine said, "I do too." (Hold up fourth finger.)
The fifth little valentine was sly as a fox. (Hold up fifth finger-pinky.)
He ran the fastest to the valentine box. (Wiggle pinkie and move hand from right to left.)

### Good Morrow to You, Valentine (Traditional, Nursery Rhyme, PreS/K–5)

Good morrow to you, Valentine!
Curl your locks as I do mine;
Two before and three behind;
Good morrow to you, Valentine!

### Good Morrow, Valentine (Traditional, Nursery Rhyme, PreS/K–5/6+)

Good morrow, Valentine!
I be thine and thou be'st mine,
So please give me a Valentine!

### Good Morrow, Valentine, God Bless You (Traditional, Nursery Rhyme, K–5/6+)

Good morrow, Valentine.
God bless you ever!
If you'll be true to me,
I'll be the like to thee.
Old England forever!

## Good Morrow, Valentine, I Go Today (Traditional, Nursery Rhyme, K–5/6+)

Good morrow, Valentine, I go today,
To wear for you what you must pay,
A pair of gloves* next Easter-day.

*During the sixteenth century, it was customary to make presents of gloves at Easter.

*See also* the "Spring" chapter, under "Spring Holidays: Easter."

## Last Valentine (Traditional, Nursery Rhyme, 6+)

Last Valentine, the day when birds of kind
Their paramours with mutual chirpings find,
I early rose, just at the break of day,
Before the sun had chased the stars away.
Afield I went, amid the burning dew,
To milk my kine,* for so should housewives do.
Thee first I spied; and the first swain** we see,
In spite of fortune shall our true love be.

*Kine: Cows.
**Swain: Young male admirer.

## Peep, Fool, Peep (Traditional, Nursery Rhyme, K–5/6+)

Peep, fool, peep,
What do you think to see?
Every one has a valentine,
And here's one for thee!

## The Rose Is Red (Traditional, Nursery Rhyme, PreS/K–5)

The rose is red,
The violet's blue;
Pinks are sweet,
And so are you!

## Sweet Guardian Angels (Traditional, Nursery Rhyme, K–5/6+)

Sweet guardian angels, let me have
What I most earnestly do crave,
A valentine endowed with love,
That will both kind and constant prove.

# Winter Weather: Snow/Ice

## Bears in a Cave (Traditional, Fingerplay, PreS/K–5)

Here is a cave. (Place right fist inside left fist.)
Inside there are bears. (Wiggle right-hand fingers under left palm.)
Now they come out (Hold right fingers up, put left hand down.)
To get some fresh air.

They stay out all summer
Its sunshine and heat.
And hunt in the forest
For berries to eat. (Mime eating berries.)

When the snow starts to fall, (Wiggle right-hand fingers over left fist.)
They hurry inside (Place right fist inside left fist again.)
Their warm little cave,
And there they will hide.

Snow covers the cave (Have right hand cover left fist.)
Like a fluffy white rug.
Inside the bears sleep,
All cozy and snug.

*See also* "Children's Song" (Ford Madox Ford, 6+) in "The Four Seasons" chapter.

## Crying, My Little One (Christina Rossetti, Poem, K–5/6+)

Crying, my little one, footsore and weary?
Fall asleep, pretty one, warm on my shoulder:
I must tramp on through the winter night dreary,
While the snow falls on me colder and colder.
You are my one, and I have not another;
Sleep soft, my darling, my trouble and treasure;
Sleep warm and soft in the arms of your mother,
Dreaming of pretty things, dreaming of pleasure.

## Dead in the Brush (Christina Rossetti, Poem, 6+)

Dead in the cold, a song-singing thrush,
Dead at the foot of a snowberry bush—
Weave him a coffin of rush,*

Dig him a grave where the soft mosses grow,
Raise him a tombstone of snow.

*Rush: A kind of marsh plant.

## February Fill the Dyke (Traditional, Nursery Rhyme, K–5/6+)

February fill the dyke,
Be it black or be it white;*
But if it be white,
It's the better to like.

*"White" refers to snow, and "black" refers to rain.

## Birds at Winter Nightfall (Thomas Hardy, Poem, 6+)

Around the house the flakes fly faster,
And all the berries now are gone
From holly and cotoneaster
Around the house. The flakes fly!—faster
Shutting indoors that crumb-outcaster
We used to see upon the lawn
Around the house. The flakes fly faster,
And all the berries now are gone!

## Fire and Ice (Robert Frost, Poem, 6+)

Some say the world will end in fire,
Some say in ice.
From what I've tasted of desire
I hold with those who favor fire.
But if it had to perish twice,
I think I know enough of hate
To say that for destruction ice
Is also great
And would suffice.

## Five Little Snowmen (Traditional, Fingerplay, PreS/K–5)

Five little snowmen happy and gay, (Show all five fingers.)
The first one said, "What a nice day." (Hold up thumb.)
The second one said, "We'll cry no tears." (Hold up second finger.)
The third one said, "We'll stay for years." (Hold up third finger.)

The fourth one said, "But what happens in May?" (Hold up fourth finger.)
The fifth one said, "Look, we're melting away." (Hold up fifth finger-pinky.)

## Five Little Snowmen (Traditional, Fingerplay, PreS/K–5)

Five little snowmen (Hold up five fingers.)
Standing in a row, Each with a hat (Touch head.)
And a big red bow. (Touch lower neck.)
One little snowman melted away. (Show one finger.)

Four little snowmen (Hold up four fingers.)
Standing in a row, Each with a hat (Touch head.)
And a big red bow. (Touch lower neck.)
One little snowman melted away. (Show one finger.)

Three little snowmen . . . (Hold up three fingers and continue with rhyme.)

Two little snowmen . . . (Hold up two fingers and continue with rhyme.)

One little snowman (Hold up one finger.)
Standing all alone,
With a hat (Touch head.)
And a big red bow. (Touch lower neck.)
Then that little snowman melted away. (Show one finger.)

## I Am a Snowman (Traditional, Fingerplay, PreS/K–5)

I am a snowman, cold and white.
I stand so still all through the night. (Stand up straight.)
With a carrot nose, (Touch nose.)
And a head held high.
And a lump of coal
To make each eye. (Touch eyes.)
I have a muffler made of red. (Touch neck.)
And a hat upon my head. (Touch head.)
The sun is coming out. Oh my! (Make a circle over head with arms.)
I think that I am going to cry. (Rub eyes.)
Yesterday, I was plump and round (Stretch out arms wide.)
Now, I'm just a river
On the ground. (Touch ground.)

*See also* "If All the Raindrops" (Traditional, PreS/K–5) in "The Four Seasons" chapter.

## Lives in Winter (Traditional, Riddle, K–5/6+)

Lives in winter,
Dies in summer,
And grows with its root upward.

Answer: An icicle.

## Merry Little Snowflakes (Traditional, Fingerplay, PreS/K–5)

Merry little snowflakes falling through the air (Flutter fingers up and down.)
Resting on the steeples and tall trees everywhere; (Stretch arms up and bring tips of the fingers together.)
Covering roofs and fences, capping every post, (Make fist with left hand and cover with right hand.)
Covering the hillside, where we like to coast. Merry little snowflakes try their very best (Flutter fingers up and down.)
To make a soft, white cover so buds and flowers may rest. (Rest hands next to head.)
When the bright spring sunshine says he's come to stay, (Make a circle over head with arms.)
Then those selfsame snowflakes quickly run away! (Fingers hide behind back.)

## The North Wind Doth Blow (Traditional, Song, PreS/K–5)

The North wind doth blow, And we shall have snow, And what will poor Ro - bin do then? He'll sit in the barn, And keep him - self warm, And tuck his head un - der his wing. Poor thing!

*See also* "Round the House" (Traditional, PreS/K–5) in "The Four Seasons" chapter, weather section.

## Plowmen (Robert Frost, Poem, K–5/6+)

I hear men say to plow the snow.
They cannot mean to plant it, though—
Unless in bitterness to mock
At having cultivated rock.

## Snow, Snow Faster (Traditional, Saying, PreS/K–5)

Snow, snow faster!*
The cow's in the pasture.

*Saying to increase snowfall.

## Snow, Snow, Give Over (Traditional, Saying, PreS/K–5)

Snow, snow, give over,*
The cow's in the clover!

*Saying to decrease snowfall.

## The Snowman (Traditional, Fingerplay, PreS/K–5)

Roll a snowball large, (Make large circle with arms.)
Then one of middle size. (Make medium-sized circle with arms.)
Roll a snowball small, (Make small circle with arms.)
Use lumps of coal for eyes. (Point to eyes.)
Place a carrot for a nose, (Point to nose.)
And an old hat on his head. (Point to head.)
And for his necktie, tie around his neck a ribbon red. (Point to neck.)
A corncob pipe goes in his mouth, (Point to mouth.)
Some buttons on his vest. (Point to tummy.)
And there he stands so round and fat, (Put hands on hips.)
Of snowmen, he's the best!

## Snow Bird (F.C. Woodworth, Poem, K–5/6+)

The ground was all covered with snow one day,
And two little sisters were busy at play
When a snow bird was sitting close by on a tree,
And merrily singing his chick-a-de-dee,
Chick-a-de-dee, chick-a-de-dee,
And merrily singing his chick-a-de-dee.

From *Big Book of Seasons, Holidays, and Weather: Rhymes, Fingerplays, and Songs for Children* by Elizabeth Cothen Low. Santa Barbara, CA: Libraries Unlimited. Copyright © 2011.

He had not been singing his tune very long
Ere Emily heard him, so loud was his song;
"Oh, sister, look out of the window," said she.
"Here's a dear little bird singing chick-a-de-dee,
Chick-a-de-dee, chick-a-de-dee,
Here's a dear little bird singing chick-a-de-dee.
"Oh, mother, do get him some stockings and shoes,
And a nice little frock, and a hat if he choose,
I wish he'd come into the parlor and see
How warm we would make him, poor chick-a-de-dee.
Chick-a-de-dee, chick-a-de-dee.
How warm we would make him, poor chick-a-de-dee."

"There is One, my dear child, though I cannot tell who,
Has clothed me already, and warm enough, too;
Good-morning! Oh, who are as happy as we?"
And away he went singing his chick-a-de-dee;
Chick-a-de-dee, chick-a-de-dee;
And away he went singing his chick-a-de-dee.

## There's Snow on the Fields (Christina Rossetti, Poem, K–5/6+)

There's snow on the fields,
And cold in the cottage,
While I sit in the chimney nook
Supping hot pottage.*
My clothes are soft and warm,
Fold upon fold,
But I'm so sorry for the poor
Out in the cold.

*Pottage: Hot stew.

## Three Children Sliding on the Ice (Traditional, Nursery Rhyme, K–5/6+)

Three children sliding on the ice,
Upon a summer's day;
It so fell out, they all fell in,
The rest they ran away.

Now had these children been at home,
Or sliding on dry ground,
Ten thousand pounds to one penny,
They had not all been drowned.

You parents that have children dear,
And eke you that have none;
If you would have them safe abroad,
Pray keep them safe at home.

## When the Snow Is on the Ground (Traditional, Song, PreS/K–5)

When the snow is on the ground, Lit-tle Ro-bin Red-breast grieves; For no ber-ries can be found, And on the trees there are no leaves. The air is cold, the worms are hid, For this poor bird what can be done? We'll strew him here some crumbs of bread, And then he'll live till the snow is gone.

# Winter: Stars

## At Night I See the Twinkling Stars (Traditional, Fingerplay, PreS/K–5)

At night I see the twinkling stars (Hold up hands and open and close, palms outward.)
And a great big smiling moon. (Make a circle over head with arms.)
My Mommy tucks me into bed (Place right index finger across left palm. Close palm over finger.)
And sings a good-night tune. (Rock hands side to side.)

## Higher Than a House (Traditional, Riddle, PreS/K–5/6+)

Higher than a house, higher than a tree;
Oh! whatever can that be?

Answer: A star.

## I Had a Little Sister (Traditional, Riddle, K–5/6+)

I had a little sister,
They called her Pretty Peep.
She wades in the waters,
Deep, deep, deep!
She climbs up the mountains,
High, high, high.
My poor little sister,
She has but one eye.

Answer: A star.

## Little Star (Traditional, Nursery Rhyme, K–5/6+)

Little star that shines so bright, come and peep at me tonight,
For I often think of you in the pretty sky so blue.
Little Star! O tell me, pray, where you hide yourself all day?

Have you got a home like me, and a father kind to see?
Little Child, at you I peep, while you lie so fast asleep.
But when dawn begins to break, I my homeward journey take.
For I've many friends on high, living with me in the sky,
And a loving Father, too,
Who commands what I'm to do.

## Star Light, Star Bright (Traditional, Nursery Rhyme, PreS/K–5)

Star light, star bright,
First star I see tonight
I wish I may, I wish I might,
Have the wish I wish tonight.

## Twinkle, Twinkle Little Star (Traditional, Song, B/PreS/K–5)

Twin - kle, twin - kle  lit - tle star,  How I won - der  what you are,

Up  a - bove  the  world  so  high,

like a dia-mond in the sky.  Twin-kle, twin-kle  lit - tle star,  How I won-der

what you are.

## Twinkle, Twinkle Little Star (Jane Taylor, Poem, B/PreS/K–5)

Twinkle, twinkle, little star,
How I wonder what you are,
Up above the world so high,
Like a diamond in the sky.
When the blazing sun is set,
And the grass with dew is wet,
Then you show your little light,
Twinkle, twinkle, all the night.
Then the traveler in the dark
Thanks you for your tiny spark,
He could not see where to go
If you did not twinkle so.
In the dark blue sky you keep,
And often through my curtains peep,
For you never shut your eye
Till the sun is in the sky.
Then the traveler in the dark
Thanks you for your tiny spark,

He could not see where to go
If you did not twinkle so.
In the dark blue sky you keep,
And often through my curtains peep,
For you never shut your eye
Till the sun is in the sky.
As your bright and tiny spark
Lights the traveler in the dark,
Though I know not what you are,
Twinkle, twinkle, little star.

# Part 2

---

## Time

The entries in this section relate to time, other than seasons and months.

# Days of the Week

## As Tommy Snooks and Bessie Brooks (Traditional, Nursery Rhyme, PreS/K-5)

As Tommy Snooks, and Bessie Brooks
Were walking out one Sunday,
Says Tommy Snooks to Bessie Brooks,
"To-morrow—will be Monday."

## Cut Your Nails On Monday (Traditional, Nursery Rhyme, K-5/6+)

Cut your nails on Monday, cut them for news;
Cut them on Tuesday, a pair of new shoes;
Cut them on Wednesday, cut them for health;
Cut them on Thursday, cut them for wealth;
Cut them on Friday, cut them for woe;
Cut them on Saturday, a journey you'll go;
Cut them on Sunday, you'll cut them for evil,
For all the next week you'll be ruled by the devil.

From *Big Book of Seasons, Holidays, and Weather: Rhymes, Fingerplays, and Songs for Children* by Elizabeth Cothen Low. Santa Barbara, CA: Libraries Unlimited. Copyright © 2011.

## How Many Days Has My Baby to Play (Traditional, Nursery Rhyme, B/PreS)

How many days has my baby to play?
Saturday, Sunday, Monday,
Tuesday, Wednesday, Thursday, Friday,
Saturday, Sunday, Monday.

## Marry Monday (Traditional, Nursery Rhyme, K-5/6+)

Marry Monday, marry for wealth;
Marry Tuesday, marry for health;
Marry Wednesday, the best day of all;
Marry Thursday, marry for crosses;
Marry Friday, marry for losses;
Marry Saturday, no luck at all.

## Monday's Child (Traditional, Nursery Rhyme, K-5/6+)

Monday's child is fair of face,
Tuesday's child is full of grace,
Wednesday's child is full of woe,
Thursday's child has far to go,
Friday's child is loving and giving,
Saturday's child works hard for its living,
And a child that's born on the Sabbath day
Is fair and wise and good and gay.

## Sneeze on a Monday (Traditional, Nursery Rhyme, K-5/6+)

Sneeze on a Monday, you sneeze for danger;
Sneeze on a Tuesday, you'll kiss a stranger;
Sneeze on a Wednesday, you sneeze for a letter;
Sneeze on a Thursday, for something better;
Sneeze on a Friday, you sneeze for sorrow;
Sneeze on a Saturday, your sweetheart to-morrow;
Sneeze on a Sunday, your safety seek—
The devil will have you the whole of the week.

## Solomon Grundy (Traditional, Nursery Rhyme, K-5/6+)

Solomon Grundy,
Born on a Monday,
Christened on Tuesday,

132

Married on Wednesday,
Took ill on Thursday,
Worse on Friday,
Died on Saturday,
Buried on Sunday,
This is the end of
Solomon Grundy.

## They That Wash on Monday (Traditional, Nursery Rhyme, K-5/6+)

They that wash on Monday
Have all the week to dry;
They that wash on Tuesday
Are not so much awry;
They that wash on Wednesday
Are not so much to blame;
They that wash on Thursday,
Wash for shame;
They that wash on Friday,
Wash in need;
They that wash on Saturday.
Oh! They are slovens indeed.

## Tomorrow Come Never (Traditional, Saying, K-5/6+)

Tomorrow come never,
When two Sundays come together.

# Hours of the Day

## Bellasay, Bellasay (Traditional, Action Rhyme, B/PreS)

Bell horses, Bell horses, what time of day?
One o'clock, two o'clock, three and away! (Pick baby up.)

## The Cock Crows in the Morn (Traditional, Nursery Rhyme, PreS/K-5)

The cock crows in the morn
To tell us to rise,
And he that lies late
Will never be wise:
For early to bed,
And early to rise,
Is the way to be healthy,
And wealthy and wise.

## The Cock Doth Crow (Traditional, Nursery Rhyme, PreS/K-5)

The cock doth crow,
To let you know,
If you be wise,
'Tis time to rise.

## A Diller, A Dollar (Traditional, Nursery Rhyme, PreS/K-5)

A diller, a dollar,
A ten o'clock scholar,
What makes you come so soon?
You used to come at ten o'clock,
But now you come at noon.

## Donkey, Donkey, Old and Gray (Traditional, Nursery Rhyme, PreS/K-5)

Donkey, donkey, old and gray,
Open your mouth and gently bray;
Lift your ears and blow your horn,
To wake the world this sleepy morn.

Donkey, donkey, do not bray,
But mend your pace and trot away.
Indeed the market's almost done,
My butter's melting in the sun.

## Elsie Marley (Traditional, Nursery Rhyme, PreS/K-5)

Elsie Marley has grown so fine,
She won't get up to serve the swine;
But lies in bed till eight or nine,
And surely she does take her time.

## He That Would Thrive (Traditional, Nursery Rhyme, K-5/6+)

He that would thrive
Must rise at five;
He that hath thriven
May lie till seven;
And he that by the plough would thrive,
Himself must either hold or drive.

## Hickory, Dickory, Dock (Traditional, Action Rhyme, Song, B/PreS/K-5)

(Also known as Dickory, Dickory, Dock or Dickery, Dickery, Dock)

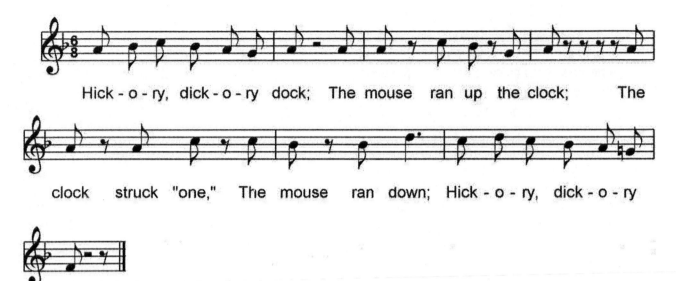

Hick - o - ry, dick - o - ry dock; The mouse ran up the clock; The

clock struck "one," The mouse ran down; Hick - o - ry, dick - o - ry

dock.

Verse 1 (includes instructions):
Hickory, dickory, dock. (Swing arm in front of you like a pendulum.)
The mouse ran up the clock, (Run fingers up arm.)
The clock struck one, (Clap hands over head once.)
The mouse ran down, (Have fingers run down arm.)
Hickory, dickory, dock. (Swing arm in front of you like a pendulum.)

## Kookoorookoo! (Christina Rossetti, Poem, PreS/K-5)

"Kookoorookoo! kookoorookoo!"
Crows the cock before the morn;
"Kikirikee! kikirikee!"
Roses in the east are born.
Kookoorookoo! kookoorookoo!"
Early birds begin their singing;
"Kikirikee! kikirikee!"
The day, the day, the day is springing.

## 'Tis Midnight (Traditional, Nursery Rhyme, K-5/6+)

'Tis midnight, and the setting sun
Is slowly rising in the west.
The rapid rivers slowly run,

The frog is on his downy nest.
The pensive goat and sportive cow,
Hilarious, leap from bough to bough.

## Morning (Jane Taylor, Poem, 6+)

The lark is up to meet the sun,
The bee is on the wing,
The ant her labor has begun,
The woods with music ring.

Shall birds and bees and ants be wise,
While I my moments waste?
Oh, let me with the morning rise,
And to my duties haste.

Why should I sleep till beams of morn
Their light and glory shed?
Immortal beings were not born
To waste their time in bed.

## Nature Requires Five (Traditional, Riddle, K-5/6+)

Nature requires five,
Custom gives seven,
Laziness takes nine,
And Wickedness eleven.

Answer: Hours of sleep.

## Robin and Richard (Traditional, Nursery Rhyme, PreS/K-5)

Robin and Richard were two pretty men;
They lay a-bed till the clock struck ten;
Then up starts Robin and looks at the sky,
"Oh! oh! brother Richard, the sun's very high,
You go before with bottle and bag,
And I'll follow after on little Jack Nag."

# Bibliography

## Websites

**Historic American Sheet Music, Duke University Libraries Digital Collection:** http://library.duke.edu/digitalcollections/hasm

**Hymns and Carols of Christmas, Douglas D. Anderson:** http://www.hymnsandcarolsofchristmas.com

**Lester S. Levy Collection of Sheet Music, Special Collections at the Sheridan Libraries of The John Hopkins University:** http://levysheetmusic.mse.jhu.edu

**Library of Congress:** http://memory.loc.gov

**Mama Lisa's World of Music, Kids Songs & International Culture, Lisa Yannucci:** http://www.mamalisa.com

**MuseScore, Free Music Composition & Notation Software:** http://musescore.org/en

**Music for the Nation: American Sheet Music:** http://memory.loc.gov/ammem/smhtml/smhome.html

**The Mutopia Project: Free Sheet Music for Everyone:** http://www.mutopiaproject.org

**NIEHS Kid's Pages, National Institutes of Environmental Health Sciences (NIEHS):** http://kids.niehs.nih.gov/music.htm

**Sheet Music Digital:** www.sheetmusicdigital.com

**Wikifonia, Wikifonia Foundation:** http://wikifonia.org

**Wikisource:** http://en.wikisource.org

**Wikipedia:** http://en.wikipedia.org/

# Books

Anonymous. 1807. *Original Ditties for the Nursery: So Wonderfully Contrived That They May Be Either Sung or Said, by Nurse or Baby.* Hockliffe Collection, 2001. http://www.cts.dmu.ac.uk/AnaServer?hockliffe+0+start.anv.

Anonymous. 1820? *Nursery Rhymes.* Hockliffe Collection, 2001. http://www.cts.dmu.ac.uk/AnaServer?hockliffe+0+start.anv.

Anonymous. 1835. *Nursery Rhymes.* Hockliffe Collection, 2001. http://www.cts.dmu.ac.uk/AnaServer?hockliffe+0+start.anv.

Anonymous. 1846. *The Book of Nursery Rhymes Complete: From the Creation of the World to the Present Time.* Google, 2006. http://books.google.com/books?id=23sAAAAAMAAJ&dq=The+book+of+nursery+rhymes+complete:+from+the+creation+of+the+world+to+the+present+time&source=gbs_navlinks_s.

Anonymous. 1850. *Old Mother Goose.* Hockliffe Collection, 2001. http://www.cts.dmu.ac.uk/AnaServer?hockliffe+0+start.anv.

Anonymous. n.d. *Mother Goose's Melody or Sonnets for the Cradle.* Hockliffe Collection, 2001. http://www.cts.dmu.ac.uk/AnaServer?hockliffe+0+start.anv.

Anonymous. *The Only True Mother Goose Melodies.* Project Gutenberg, 2004. http://www.gutenberg.org/etext/4901.

Beall, Pamela Conn and Susan Hagen Nipp. *Wee Sing Nursery Rhymes & Lullabies.* Los Angeles: Price Stern Sloan, 1985.

Beall, Pamela Conn and Susan Hagen Nipp. *Wee Sing: Children's Songs and Fingerplays.* New York: Price Stern Sloan, 2005.

Belloc, Hilaire. 1897. *More Beasts for Worse Children.* Baldwin Online Children's Literature Project, 2000-2008. http://www.mainlesson.com/display.php?author=belloc&book=more&story=_contents.

Belloc, Hilaire. 1896. *The Bad Child's Book of Beasts.* Baldwin Online Children's Literature Project, 2000-2008. http://www.mainlesson.com/display.php?author=belloc&book=beasts&story=_contents.

Brooke, L. Leslie, ill. 1922. *Ring O' Roses: A Nursery Rhyme Picture Book.* Project Gutenberg, 2007.

Brown, Florence Warren and Neva L. Boyd. *Old English and American Games for School and Playground.* Chicago: H.T. FitzSimons Company, 1915.

Cheviot, Andrew. 1896. *Proverbs, Proverbial Expressions, and Popular Rhymes of Scotland.* Google Books, 2005. http://books.google.com/books?id=XsC6Dy8A2d4C.

Cooper, Kay. *Too Many Rabbits: and Other Fingerplays about Animals, Nature, Weather, and the Universe.* New York: Scholastic, 1995.

Cooper, Kay. *The Neal-Schuman Index to Finger-plays.* New York: Neal-Schuman Publishers, Inc., 1993.

Curry, Charles Madison. 1921. *Children's Literature: A Textbook of Sources for Teachers and Teacher.* Google Books, 2007. http://books.google.com/books?id=_nJAAAAAIAAJ.

Delamar, Gloria T. *Children's Counting-Out Rhymes, Fingerplays, Jump-Rope and Bounce-Ball Chants and Other Rhythms, A Comprehensive English-Language Reference.* Jefferson, N.C.: McFarland, 1983.

Elliot, J.W. *National Nursery Rhymes and Nursery Songs.* London: Novello and Company, 1870.

Fowke, Edith. *Sally Go Round the Sun: Three Hundred Children's Songs, Rhymes and Games.* Garden City, N.Y.: Doubleday and Company, Inc., 1969.

Glazer, Tom. Do *Your Ears Hang Low?: Fifty More Musical Fingerplays.* Garden City, N.Y.: Doubleday & Company, Inc., 1980.

Glazer, Tom. *Eye Winker, Tom Tinker, Chin Chopper: Fifty Musical Fingerplays.* Garden City, N.Y.: Doubleday & Company, Inc., 1973.

Glazer, Tom. *Mother Goose Songbook.* New York: Doubleday, 1990.

Grayson, Marion. *Let's Do Fingerplays.* Wash.: Robert B. Luce, 1962.

Greenaway, Kate. *Kate Greenaway's Mother Goose.* San Marino, Calif.: Huntington Library Press, 2006.

Greenwald, Celia. *Children's Games with Words.* New York: The Empire Music Co., 1907.

Halliwell, James Orchard. 1886. *Nursery Rhymes of England.* Google Books, 2007. http://books.google.com/books?id=0jcDAAAAYAAJ.

Halliwell, James Orchard. 1849. *Popular Rhymes and Nursery Tales.* Google Books, 2008. http://books.google.com/books?id=pFmBAAAAMAAJ&ots.

Newell, William Wells. *Games and Songs of American Children.* New York: Harper & Brothers, Pub., 1888.

Opie, Iona and Peter Opie, eds. *Oxford Dictionary of Nursery Rhymes.* rev. ed. Oxford, UK: Oxford University Press, 1997.

Poulsson, Emilie and Cornelia C. Roeske. *Finger-Plays for Nursery and Kindergarten.* Boston: Lothrop, Lee, and Shepard, Co., 1893. Also available online at http://books.google.com/books?id=oBU1WmAYGV0C.

Rossetti, Christina Georgina. *Sing-Song: A Nursery Rhyme Book.* rev. ed. New York: MacMillan and Co., 1893. Also available at http://digital.library.upenn.edu/women/rossetti/singsong/singsong.html.

Skinner, Ada M., and Frances Gillespy Wickes. 1917. *A Child's Own Book of Verse, Book One.* Baldwin Online Children's Literature Project, 2000-2008. http://www.mainlesson.com/display .php?author=skinner&book=verse1&story=_contents.

Smith, Eleanor. *Songs for Little Children: Part 1, A Collection of Songs and Games for Kindergartens and Primary Schools*. Springfield, Mass.: Milton Bradley Co., 1887.

Smith, Jessie Willcox, illus. 1918. *The Little Mother Goose*. Project Gutenberg, 2007. http://www .gutenberg.org/ebooks/20511.

Stevenson, Burton Egbert. 1912. The Home Book of Verse, Volume 1. Project Gutenberg, 2009. http://www.gutenberg.org/ebooks/2619.

Stevenson, Robert Louis. *A Child's Garden of Verses*. Project Gutenberg, 1994. http://www.gutenberg .org/dirs/etext94/child11.txt.

Wells, Carolyn, ed. 1910. *A Nonsense Anthology*. Google Books, 2007. http://books.google.com/ books?id=_jQNAAAAYAAJ.

Wicklund, Brian. *American Fiddle Method*. Pacific, Mo.: Mel Bay Publications, 2001.

Wier, Albert E. *Songs the Children Love to Sing*. New York: D. Appleton and Company, 1916.

Wildsmith, Brian. *Nursery Rhymes Mother Goose*. Oxford, UK: Oxford University Press, 1964.

## Supplemental Works

Fishman, Stephen. *The Public Domain: How to Find & Use Copyright-Free Writings, Music, Art & More*. Berkeley, Calif.: Nolo, 2000.

Lima, Carolyn W., and John A. Lima. *A to Zoo: Subject Access to Children's Picture Books*. Westport, Conn.: Bowker-Greenwood, 2001.

Summerly, Felix, ed. *The Home Treasury: Traditional Nursery Songs of England*. London: Joseph Cundall, 1843.

Zimmerman, Barbara. *The Mini-Encyclopedia of Public Domain Songs*. New York: BZ/Rights Stuff, 1997.

# Author Index

# Title Index

# First Line Index

A diller, a dollar, 136
A frisky lamb, 61
A hill full, a hole full, 88
A little boy went walking, 58
All hail to the moon, all hail to thee!, 83
A man of words, and not of deeds, 28
A man of words and not of deeds, 27
And so they went along, 79
And where have you been, my Mary, 54
A northern har, 88
An owl sat alone on the branch of a tree, 81
April-fool time's past and gone, 31
A red sky at night is a shepherd's delight, 9
Around the house the flakes fly faster, 120
Arthur O' Bower has broken his band, 42
As I was going to Banbury, 53
As I went through the garden gap, 73
As Tommy Snooks, and Bessie Brooks, 131
As the days grow longer, 35
A sunshiny shower, 41
A swarm of bees in May, 6
As white as milk, 19
A tiny moon as white and small as a single jasmine
    flower, 31
At night I see the twinkling stars, 125
At the end of my yard there is a vat, 73
A water there is I must pass, 41
Away in a manger, 99

Banks full, braes full, 88
Bell horses, Bell horses, what time of day?, 135
Blow, wind, blow!, 98
Blow the wind high, blow the wind low, 43
Bobbin-a-Bobbin bent his bow, 54
Bounce Buckram, velvet's dear, 99
Bread and milk for breakfast, 91

Care Sunday, 32
Catch him, crow! Carry him, kite!, 74
Christmas comes but once a year, 99
Christmas is coming, the geese are getting fat, 100
Cold and raw the north wind doth blow, 91
Crying, my little one, footsore and weary?, 119
Cuckoo, cuckoo, 3
Cuckoo, cuckoo, cherry tree, 75

Cuckoo, cuckoo, pretty bird say, 13
Cut your nails on Monday, cut them for news, 131

Dame, get up and bake your pies, 100
Dashing through the snow, 104
Dead in the cold, a song-singing thrush, 119
Deck the halls with boughs of holly, 101
Doctor Foster went to Gloucester, 35
Donkey, donkey, old and gray, 136
Double Dee Double Day, 20
Down in a green and shady bed, 30
Do you ask what the birds say? The Sparrow, the
    Dove, 11
Draw a pail of water, 21

Easter Bunny's ears are floppy, 32
Elsie Marley has grown so fine, 136
Evening red and morning gray, 37

February fill the dyke, 120
Five Little Goblins on a Halloween night, 80
Five fat turkeys are we, 81
Five little Easter eggs lovely colors wore, 32
Five little Pilgrims on Thanksgiving Day, 81
Five little bells, hanging in a row, 103
Five little busy bees on a day so sunny, 60
Five little flowers standing in the sun, 21
Five little pumpkins sitting on a gate, 80
Five little snowmen, 121 (Hold up five fingers.)
Five little snowmen happy and gay, 120
Five little valentines were having a race, 117
Flowers tall, flowers small, 21
Fly away, fly away over the sea, 67
Four Seasons fill the measure of the year, 5

Gay little Dandelion, 24
Girls and boys, come out to play, 83
God bless the master of this house, 104
Good morning, missus and master, 33
Good morrow, Valentine!, 117
Good morrow, Valentine, I go today, 118
Good morrow, Valentine, 117
Good morrow, my lord! in the sky alone, 64
Good morrow to you, Valentine!, 117
Go tell it on the mountain, 103

149

# Specific Kinds of Rhymes

**Riddles**

# About the Author

ELIZABETH COTHEN LOW is the author of *Big Book of Animal Rhymes, Fingerplays, and Songs* (Libraries Unlimited, 2009). She has an MLS from the University of Illinois and has worked as a children's librarian. She currently lives in Queens with her husband and two young children.